ISSUES IN SPANISH MORPHOPHONOLOGY

Implications for Language Acquisition

Obdulia Castro

University Press of America,® Inc.
Lanham · Boulder · New York · Toronto · Oxford

Copyright © 2006 by
University Press of America,® Inc.
4501 Forbes Boulevard
Suite 200
Lanham, Maryland 20706
UPA Acquisitions Department (301) 459-3366

PO Box 317
Oxford
OX2 9RU, UK

All rights reserved
Printed in the United States of America
British Library Cataloging in Publication Information Available

Library of Congress Control Number: 2006926773

ISBN-13: 978-0-7618-3531-8 (paperback : alk. paper)
ISBN-10: 0-7618-3531-8 (paperback : alk. paper)

∞™ The paper used in this publication meets the minimum
requirements of American National Standard for Information
Sciences—Permanence of Paper for Printed Library Materials,
ANSI Z39.48—1984

Table of Contents

List of Figures	iv
List of Tables	v
Preface	vii
I. Trubetzkoy's Orphan Revisited: A View from Spanish Morphophonology	1
II. Overview of Optimality Theory	7
III. Spanish Morphophonology and Language Acquisition	13
IV. Stress and Intonation	33
V. The Obligatory Contour Principle and the Pronoun System of Spanish: Syntax, Morphology, and Phonology at the Crossroads	51
VI. The Acquisition of Alternating Diphthongs in Native and Non-Native Systems	57
VII. Inflection vs. Derivation	69
VIII. Phonological Processing and Foreign Language Learning Difficulties	95
IX. Addressing Language Learnability: How Much Information is Enough for Learning Systems to be Successful? Galician *geada* and Catalan *queada*	105
Appendix I	115
Appendix II	137
Bibliography	141
Author/Subject Index	149
About the Author	151

List of Figures

Figure 4.1.	Intensity Chart for *Se puso a hablar conmigo* "He engaged me in conversation" uttered by a non-Galician Spanish speaker	42
Figure 4.2.	Intensity Chart for *Se puso a hablar conmigo* "He engaged me in conversation" uttered by a Galician Spanish speaker	43
Figure 4.3.	Spectrogram for *Se puso a hablar conmigo* "He engaged me in conversation" uttered by a Spanish speaker	43
Figure 4.4.	Spectrogram for *Se puso a hablar conmigo* "He engaged me in conversation" uttered by a Galician Spanish speaker	43
Figure 4.5.	Pitch Chart for *Se puso a hablar conmigo* "He engaged me in conversation" uttered by a Spanish speaker	44
Figure 4.6.	Pitch Chart for *Se puso a hablar conmigo* "He engaged me in conversation" uttered by a Galician Spanish speaker	44
Figure 4.7.	Pitch Chart of *como non ves...* "Since you are not coming..." uttered by a Galician speaker	45
Figure 4.8.	Pitch Chart of *como no vienes...* "Since you are not coming..." uttered by a non-Galician speaker	45
Figure 4.9.	Pitch Contour for *¿Cómo non ves?* "What do you mean you are not coming?" uttered by a Galician speaker	46
Figure 4.10.	Pitch Contour for *¿Cómo que no vienes?* "What do you mean you are not coming?" uttered by a Spanish monolingual speaker	46
Figure 4.11.	Pitch Contour of *¿Cómo que no vienes?* "What do you mean you are not coming?" uttered by a bilingual Galician speaker	47
Figure 4.12.	Pitch Contour of *¿Cómo no vienes?* "What do you mean you are not coming?" uttered by a bilingual Galician Spanish speaker	47

List of Tables

Table 3.1.	Possible Constraint Rankings for *mecánica* "mechanic" (fem.) (adj.)	17
Table 3.2.	Possible Rankings for *Madrid* (proper name)	20
Table 3.3.	Syllables with Coda	22
Table 3.4.	Sample of Number of Syllables at One Year	23
Table 3.5.	Syllable Structure: Consonants	26
Table 3.6.	Consonants in Coda Position in Andalusian Spanish	27
Table 3.7.	Possible Rankings for *los osos* "bears"	28
Table 3.8.	Possible Rankings for *algún* "some" (masc.)	29
Table 3.9.	Possible Rankings for *algunha* "some" (fem.) (Galician)	30
Table 3.10.	Possible Rankings for *alguna* "some" (fem.) (Spanish)	30
Table 4.1.	Acquisition of Stress in L2	37
Table 5.1.	Hypothetical Evolution of *illis illum* to *se lo*	53
Table 6.1.	Native Acquisition of Alternating Diphthongs *e–ie*	60
Table 6.2.	Native Acquisition of Alternating Diphthongs *o–ue*	61
Table 6.3.	Native Percentage of Target Forms 1-3 Years	61
Table 6.4.	Comparison of Percentage of Target Forms for *ie* and *ue*	62
Table 6.5.	Production of Forms with Alternating Diphthongs, 1:07-2:01	62
Table 6.6:	Native System from 1:07-2:01, % of Target/Non-Target Forms	63
Table 6.7.	L2 Acquisition of Alternating Diphthongs (First Semester)	63
Table 6.8.	Comparison of Totals vs. Target Forms in L2	64
Table 6.9.	Sample Results for [ew] in the First-Semester Group	65
Table 6.10.	Sample Results for [ew] in the Third-Year Group	65
Table 6.11.	Results for [ew] in the First-Semester Group	65
Table 6.12.	Results for [ew] in the Third-Year Group	66
Table 6.13.	[jo] First Semester	67
Table 6.14.	[jo] Third Year	67
Table 7.1.	Possible Rankings for *mesa* "table" (fem.)	76
Table 7.2.	Possible Rankings for *calor* "heat" (masc.)	77
Table 7.3.	Possible Rankings for *papel* "paper" (masc.)	77

Table 7.4.	Possible Rankings for *madre* "mother" (fem.)	78
Table 7.5.	Possible Rankings for *camión* "truck" (masc.)	78
Table 7.6.	Possible Rankings for *lápiz* "pencil" (masc.)	78
Table 7.7.	Possible Rankings for *río* "river" (masc.)	79
Table 7.8.	Possible Rankings for *leona* "lioness" (fem.)	80
Table 7.9.	Possible Rankings for *tapia* "stone (adobe, mud, etc.) decorative and/or protective outside wall or fence" (fem.)	80
Table 7.10.	Possible Rankings for *rey* "king" (masc.)	81
Table 7.11.	Foot and Syllable Structure: *casa–casita*	82
Table 7.12.	Possible Rankings for *reina* "queen" (fem.)	83
Table 7.13.	Possible Rankings for *bueno* "good" (masc.) (adj.)	83
Table 7.14.	Possible Rankings for *piedra* "stone" (fem.)	84
Table 7.15.	Possible Rankings for *piano* "piano" (masc.)	85
Table 7.16.	Possible Rankings for *mal* "evil" (masc.)	85
Table 7.17.	Possible Rankings for *malo* "bad" (masc.)	86
Table 7.18.	Possible Rankings for *Carlos* "Charles" (masc.)	86
Table 7.19.	Possible Rankings for *mapa* "map" (masc.)	87
Table 7.20.	Possible Rankings for *mano* "hand" (fem.)	87
Table 7.21.	Possible Rankings for *policía* "policeman" (masc.)	89
Table 7.22.	Spanish Gender for English Words	92
Table 7.23.	Assignment of Spanish Gender to English Words	93
Table 8.1.	Pronunciation of Target /b/	97
Table 8.2.	Forms Encountered in the Third-Year Group	97
Table 8.3.	*Eusebio* (masc.) (proper name)	98
Table 8.4.	Syllable Identification	99
Table 8.5.	Sample Results for [β] in Third-Year Group (based on number of samples)	99
Table 8.6.	Forms Encountered in the First-Semester Group	101
Table 8.7.	*Eusebio* (masc.) (proper name)	101
Table 8.8.	Results for [β] in First-Semester Group	103
Table 9.1.	Re-Interpretation of Castilian /x/ in Galician and Catalan	108
Table 9.2.	Summary of OT Constraints	110
Table 9.3.	Castilian System	110
Table 9.4.	Castilian System (within a phrase)	111
Table 9.5.	Castilian System (preceded by a nasal)	111
Table 9.6.	Galician System with *geadas*	111
Table 9.7.	Galician System with *geadas* (within a phrase)	112
Table 9.8.	Galician System with *geadas* (preceded by a nasal sound)	112
Table 9.9.	Galician without *geada*	112
Table 9.10.	A Look at *gueadas* within Galician	113
Table 9.11.	The Catalan System	113

Preface

Based on data from L1 and L2 environments in Spanish language acquisition, this study examines syllable structure, stress assignment, alternating diphthongs, phonological processing, and other linguistic phenomena occurring mostly in the interface between phonology and morphology in Spanish. In order to study this morphophonological interaction, this book takes both an empirical and theoretical approach to the study of Spanish language acquisition both in native and non-native systems, subsequently identifying similarities and differences in learnability between both systems.

Recent studies in Optimality Theory (OT) (Prince and Smolensky, 1993) have pointed out the similarities between the processes of language change and language learning (Holt, 1997; Anttila and Cho, 1998; Morris, 2000; Adam, 2002). Language change or variation has been studied within OT as being motivated by re-ranking, partial ranking (Anttila, 1995; Adam, 2002) or un-ranking, and/or variable ranking of faithfulness constraints. By considering language change as a part of language learning, we explain why language change, although always present, is not rampant, as languages do not change as rapidly as it could be expected. They remain surprisingly stable considering the possibilities from both diachronic and synchronic perspectives.

The articles in this book argue that, although the same constraints are expected to play a role in both language learning and language change, these processes are not to be confused. OT Faithfulness constraints are violated frequently with theoretical predictability in language learning. In language change, they are still violated, but to a lesser degree. At the beginning stages of both native and non-native learning systems, a larger number of possible output candidates are generated than at more advanced stages. Nevertheless, when comparing native and non-native learning systems, fewer candidates are generated in non-native environments at both stages of language development.

Although this study tends to agree with Martinet (1965), in not considering the problems encompassed by morphophonology of such great uniqueness as to dictate the creation of a new discipline; it does consider the study of these phenomena of significant importance within the field of linguistics. As such, they deserve to be given a considerable greater degree of attention, as in the past they have been, more often than not, discarded as a sideline of language typology. Already in 1978, Cressey hinted to this need by including morphology in his book on Spanish phonology, but besides Dressler (1985), and Singh (1996) there has not been any comprehensive study of morphophonology related issues in recent years. In this book we look at morphophonology following a paradigm close to the one suggested by Tiffou (1994), where although morphophonology is not seen as a linguistic domain proper, it is looked at as a dynamic principle regulating the relationships between phonology and morphology. In any case, looking at these sometimes easy and sometimes overtly difficult to explain phenomena, we hope to help explaining the nature of morphology itself and its relationship with phonology, which has driven Aronoff (1998) to consider it a disease. In his own words morphology is "an unnatural mapping between components," referring to the continuous overlapping of morphology with both phonology and syntax. This book aims to modestly contribute to a better understanding of these relationships.

Obdulia Castro
Lafayette, Colorado
April, 2006

I.
Trubetzkoy's Orphan Revisited: A View from Spanish Morphophonology

The concept of morphophonology is deeply entrenched between the notions of diachronic and synchronic language development. What we today consider to be irregular forms in language learning involve phenomena that often respond to historical processes in language development. The question that remains to be answered is how much of the history of the language does the speaker (learner) need to know (if any) in order to produce and/or control these forms.

Some of the linguistic phenomena that appear to be formed in the interface between morphology and phonology have been discussed and studied for a number of years. Bybee (1994) considers these phenomena "fossilized sound change from bygone eras." Bybee also believes that "a fundamental problem for morphophonology is distinguishing between diachronic residue routinized in words in the lexicon and synchronically viable patterns" (1991, 247). Examples as productive as gender marking and diminutive and plural formation in Spanish help us identify those processes involved that are actually fossilized, as well as those that are still very much alive and accessible to learners. One good example of this would be the good number of words in Spanish that have a single vowel alternating with a diphthong depending on the position of the stress: (*e–ie: tener* "to have" – *tiene* "he, she, it has, you (formal) have"; *o–ue: poder* "to be able to" – *puede* "he, she, it can, you (formal) can." Some of these words have two possible forms of the diminutive, i.e., *puente* "bridge" → *puentito/puentecito* "small bridge," *puerto* "port" → *puertito /puertecito* "small port," *diente* "tooth" → *dientito/dientecito* "small tooth." While other forms that could also be candidates for this alternation like *abuelo* "grand father" → *abuelito* "grandpa"[1] and *piano* "piano" → *pianito* "small piano" do not. This can be seen as an indication that speakers do not interpret *abuelo* and *piano* as containing an alternating diphthong. Furthermore, the speakers who pronounce *puentito* seem to be using a different syllable and/or foot structure than the ones who pronounce *puente-*

cito. Alternating diphthongs, although certainly an example of historical development, give us great insight into the current structure of Spanish words as we study language learnability.

Forms such as *tener* "to have" – *tiene* "he, she, it has; you (formal) have"; *dormir* "to sleep" – *duermo* "I sleep"; *festejar* "to celebrate" – *fiesta* "party, celebration," *amoblar/amueblar* "to furnish" – *muebles* "furniture" – *mobiliario* "furnishings" show an alternation where the vowels *e* and *o* appear in the same contexts as *ie* and *ue*, the only difference being the placement of stress: unstressed *e* and *o* vs. stressed *ie* and *ue*.[2] In the first-language-learner-system, the non-target form *tene* co-exists with the target *tiene* "he, she it has; you (formal) have" for a short period of time, but we have no examples of forms such as **tiénemos* for *tenemos* "we have." It seems that the vowel -and not the diphthong- is acquired first for the whole paradigm. In the foreign-language-learner-system, we find that the possibility of production of target-like forms increases with form familiarity, but we observe a period of non-target forms of the type **tienémos–tiénemos* instead of the target *tenemos*. This suggests that the vowel seems to be the optimal candidate for the first language learner during the beginning stages of the learning process, while both vowel and diphthong compete for higher ranking during the inter-language period of foreign/second language learners (L2 learners).

Two important ideas that are examined throughout this book are language change and language learning. Although some constraints that are present in language learning play a role in language change,[3] these two processes are not to be confused. In language learning, we find that Optimality Theory (OT) faithfulness constraints are frequently violated. This is to be expected, as there is not a fixed form to follow yet. We see in both native and non-native learning systems, that at the beginning of the learning process we have a larger number of candidates than at more advanced stages.[4] Nevertheless, there are fewer candidates within the native learning system. Language change and/or variation can be considered within OT as being motivated by a lower or variable ranking of faithfulness constraints. In language change, faithfulness constraints are still violated but to a lesser degree than in L2 learning. This explains why language change, although always present, is not rampant; in other words, languages do not change as rapidly as could be expected. They remain surprisingly stable from a diachronic perspective considering the possibilities.

Morphophonology has been a source of controversy for a number of scholars who have studied the nature of this phenomenon through the years. The origins of the disputed placement of morphophonology within the main components of the linguistic system can be traced back to Trubetzkoy (1929, 1931, 1939),[5] who saw this discipline as part of both phonology and morphology. From that point on, linguists at different times have considered parts of morphophonology as belonging to either phonology or morphology,[6] or even as a good number of Russian scholars did, as a totally separate component. On the other hand, Dressler (1985) sees it as belonging neither to phonology, or morphology, while not forming a separate component by itself either.

Linguists of the Prague Circle relegated everything that could not be expressed or explained through rules to the field of morphophonology. Chomsky and Halle (1968) included what we call morphophonology within phonology while trying to explain the processes affected by it as regular derivations through the specification of deep structures and synchronic rules. As postulated by Chomsky and Halle, this vision of morphophonological processes was one of the great advances of traditional generative phonology, but it quickly became one of its most difficult problems. Their efforts to explain forms like the English *go–went* as regular derivations, and to include processes such as this within the regular phonology, represented a sincere and brave attempt to recognize active patterns in apparent unexplainable peculiarities of language arrived at through historical evolution. This approach was also applied to explain Spanish forms like *tengo* "I have" as a regular derivation from the underlying structure *teneo*. Therefore, the implication was that native speakers had this form as their underlying representation or deep structure, and consequently made these connections as part of their active linguistic knowledge. Traditional generative phonologists ran into serious problems establishing as underlying structures forms that did not exist in any shape or form in real language. This distance from deep structure to surface structure in traditional generative phonology gave way to the emergence of Natural Phonology (Hooper, 1976), where deep structures were highly restrained through the requirement that they have some level of possible relationship to surface forms. What we gained in transparency, we lost in the generalization and abstract conceptualization of derivations.

One of the most important developments in the treatment of the interleaving of phonology and morphology has been the introduction of lexical phonology by Kiparsky (1982). In this approach, phonology and morphology belong in the same module because phonological and morphological information must be present at the same time. The awareness of this different behavior in the application of lexical and post-lexical rules was one of the most revealing findings of this theory, together with the consideration of the lexicon as a level-ordered and rule-organized entity. Theories like OT have to be able to account for all the processes that were explained within Lexical Phonology.

There is little discussion about the independent nature of phonology, morphology, and syntax, but morphophonology has been claimed to be a part of all these components. We have mentioned so far the interaction between morphology and phonology, but interestingly enough, morphology has also been connected with syntax to form what has been called morphosyntax. Referring to Givon (1979), Bybee (1994) states that one of the reasons morphology is frequently related with syntax is that morphology is "old syntax" given that affixes were at one point in time independent words. We can see that both morphology and morphophonology have been explained as having a close relationship with historical processes. Trying to discern what historical processes are no longer active—and which ones are still a part of the synchronic state of the language—is one of the main objectives of this book. This is one of the reasons we decided to look at phonological processing and learning difficulties. Learning difficulties are conceptualized in two distinct ways in this book. On the one hand, we look at difficulties intrinsic to the learner; on the other hand, we look at difficulties intrinsic to the learning environment or situation. In this particular instance we study the situation of Galician and Spanish in contact and examine how this contact has affected language learning on both sides.

Although the existence of morphology as a separate component of the linguistic system is not in doubt, Anderson (1992), in his *A-Morphous Morphology*, and Ford and Singh (1994), in what they call Projection Morphology, consider that words are not formed by morphemes or morphs. For them, the notion of morpheme and the internal syntactic composition of words have no part in morphology. According to these authors, speakers limit themselves to adding endings of an unspecified nature to words, and once the new word is formed, they have no access to any internal constituents (morphological or phonological). However, native speakers and learners alike can make correct predictions about the nature of affixes that can be added to words, or about the nature of transformations that words can undergo.

Most studies about diminutives in Spanish (Carreira, 1985; Castro, 1998; Harris, 1980-1983; Jaeggli, 1981) generally agree that the input to form the diminutive is the whole word, including information about gender and the terminal element: *papel* "paper" → *papelito* "small paper," *carro* "car" → *carrito* "small car," etc. Nevertheless, forms like *(el) mapa* "map," without exception, form the diminutive as *(el) mapita* "small map," copying the last vowel of the original word, and not **el mapito*, maintaining the gender of the original word. It seems that the speaker needs to have more information available besides the gender and terminal element.[7] After Harris (1991a, 1991b), we know that final –*a* in words like *mapa* is not the gender marker, but a word marker. Thus, this clearly suggests that the speaker knows, or has access to, morphological information.

Words ending in –*n* form the diminutive with the allomorph –*cit* instead of –*it*. It seems there is a prosodic constraint according to which the –*n* cannot be re-syllabified as part of the onset (beginning of the next syllable) after it has been assigned to the rhyme (end of the syllable). This is true for most of the Spanish-speaking world, with the exception of the Canary Islands, where the diminutive of words like *pan* "bread" and *pantalón* "pants" are *panito* and *pantalonito* respectively, an indication that the previous constraint appears to no longer apply. It seems apparent that native speakers have access to the notion of syllable. Nevertheless, the syllable was one of the constructs thrown out of Sound Pattern of English (SPE) because it was thought not to have any real function. For one, it is not possible to make a list of real syllables in a language, while we can come up with a list of real morphemes. Languages like Spanish are a clear example of the need to consider the syllable a legitimate and necessary object of study.

The words *Ascona* (a type of car) and *Pamplona* (the name of a city) have *Asconita* and *Pamplonita* as their diminutives, while words like *llorona* "female person given to weeping" and *copiona* "female copycat" form their diminutives as *lloroncita* and *copioncita*. It seems that the speaker has access to more information than previously thought: the latter words are inflected with the suffix *–on* to form affective augmentatives, while the former two words are presumably derived locatives. These derived locatives are already lexicalized, and therefore, not currently productive, although speakers recognize them as suffixes.[8] What is interesting about the diminutive forms mentioned here is that they seem to use the masculine form of the word as the base for the masculine as well as the feminine diminutive.

The affixation of *–s* to form the plural in Spanish seems to be a straightforward process with no apparent complications. Nevertheless, even non-native proficient speakers of the language encounter difficulty when forming the plural of words like *"standard,"* which has been adapted from English into Spanish as *estándar,* although both forms still coexist. The native English speaker sees a *–d* at the end of the original word and proceeds to form the plural following the pattern for words like *verdad* "truth" → *verdades, pared* "wall" → *paredes,* producing **estandardes*. Native speakers of Spanish, on the other hand, are aware of the fact that *–rd* is not a possible consonant cluster in word final position in Spanish and delete the final *–d* before affixation. Therefore, the base for plural affixation in Spanish is the form *estándar,* giving the correct plural for this word: *estándares*.

Consonants at the beginning or end of syllables and/or words in Spanish undergo a number of changes. Among the most studied are the fairly stable but variable final *s* deletion or aspiration where a word like *casas* "houses" can be pronounced [kasa], [kasah], or [kasas] based on different conditioning sociolinguistic factors; the fairly regular and stable nasal assimilation where words like *diente* "tooth" are regularly pronounced with a dentalized *–n* [djen̪te] due to the assimilation of the nasal to the point of articulation of the dental [t]; and nasal velarization where the nasal at the end of word or syllable is pronounced as a velar. This can be the result of a regular assimilation process, as in the previous case, or a variable conditioning of final position. In this latter case all nasals at the end of a syllable and/or word can be pronounced as a velar as in *cantan* "they, you (formal) sing" pronounced as [kan̪taŋ]. Based on a variety of corpus data, this study looks at final *–s* deletion/aspiration and *–n* assimilation and velarization as examples of preservation of the optimal syllable structure in Spanish.

In order to attempt to give an explanation for the previous data, we need to be able to refer to concepts such as the morpheme; specifically, "the diminutive morpheme" and the "gender morpheme." We also need to make reference to the syllable, to syllable structure and to the boundaries at the end of both words and syllables, as well as to the internal structure of words. It is obvious that the speaker needs to have access to at least part of this information. Nevertheless, Kiparsky (1994), while accepting the internal structure of words, questions the need for the concept of morpheme. This could apply to languages without morphology, or to languages with lower levels of morphological processes, but not necessarily to languages with highly developed morphology. Examples from

Spanish indicate that speakers have access to the internal structure of words and to morphological concepts such as morphemes and roots.

Within the last ten years, a growing field of information in Optimality Theory has emerged with new versions of OT. This enables us to have a fresh look at the position of morphophonological phenomena within the linguistic system. OT, with its list of universal but violable constraints, has developed a new hypothesis about the morphology-phonology relationship. McCarthy and Prince (1993) consider that, once morphemes have been lexically specified, the input generator (GEN) should not affect them. This means that changes like epenthesis and/or deletion will not affect the morphological shape of a morpheme, although they can affect its phonetic shape. This seems to indicate that concepts such as affix need to be a part of the linguistic description.

Notes

1. Although the term "diminutive" seems to refer to the idea of smallness, this is not always the case, as the use of this form more often than not makes an emotional comment on the relationship of the object and/or person mentioned and the speaker. In the case of *abuelito*, the diminutive is a marker to the special relationship between the speaker and the grandfather, and it should not be interpreted as "small grandfather" but rather as "grandpa."

2. Notice that *amueblar* "furnish" does not have *ue* in stressed position, as the stress falls in the last syllable for the infinitive form of verbs.

3. See examples from Galician Spanish.

4. See the chapters on syllable acquisition and alternating diphthongs.

5. But as Singh (1996) reminds us, this term was originally created at the end of the nineteenth century by a neo-grammarian called Henryk Ulaszyn.

6. See Dressler (1985) and Kilbury (1976) for a complete review.

7. Words like *la mano* "hand" have two possible forms in the diminutive: *la manito*, maintaining the original –*o*, and *la manita*, introducing the feminine marker. The former is typical of Spain, while the latter is frequently heard in Latin America.

8. Such was the case of a Spanish child who jokingly asked the owner of an Ascona *¿Cómo puedes tener un coche que es un asco?* "How can you have a car that is repulsive?" Of course this is a play on words using the word *asco* (disgust, repulsion) as the base form and adding the augmentative suffix –*on(a)* to come up with the apparently derived form *Ascona*. Of course, we do not imagine that that was the intent of the company that named the car.

II.
Overview of Optimality Theory

Optimality Theory, according to Prince and Smolensky (1993), has developed a way to analyze and describe phonological processes on a constraint-based theory. According to OT, a grammar is a set of universal constraints that are part of Universal Grammar. These constraints are present in all languages, and differences between languages are explained by the different ranking of these constraints. One major advance made by this theory is the fact that these constraints are violable. A set of candidate output forms is produced by the Generator (GEN) and processed by the Evaluator (EVAL), which determines the output satisfaction to the constraint hierarchy and its optimality. OT presents itself as an option to rule-based theories that used constraints and filters to explain different outputs.

McCarthy (1995) advanced OT by incorporating what it is now called Correspondence Theory, according to which there is a group of constraints called "faithfulness constraints," which are:

1. MAX: The surface form should maximally retain underlying features or segments (it replaces PARSE in the Prince and Smolensky framework). This constraint says that no feature or segment should be deleted.

2. IDENT(ity)-[F]: input and output segments have the same values for a particular feature, place, etc.

3. DEP(endency) (FILL in Prince and Smolensky's framework): Output forms should depend on underlying forms. This constraint prevents insertion or epenthesis.

According to Correspondence Theory, faithfulness violations are assessed directly by examining the relation between the input and output.

Morphophonology in OT

Since SPE, the idea that the different modules of the grammar are distinct and ought to be kept separate has dominated the studies in the field. The correction of specific forms was determined based on their correctness in each grammar module. The principle of phonology-free syntax derives directly from this idea. According to this principle, syntax can influence phonology, but no phonologically determined process can affect syntax. Linguistic phenomena where two or more modules seemed to interact, or where phonology seemed to dominate syntax (see Yip, 1998; Perlmutter, 1998), found no explanation within this view of the organization of grammar.

Although further research needs to be done, OT offers the possibility of stipulating a ranking order of constraints where a phonological constraint would be ranked higher than a syntactic one, as in the example presented by Perlmutter (1998), where the Obligatory Contour Principle (OCP), a phonological constraint, outranks CONCORD, a syntax-based constraint. The possibility of constraints from a specific module to outrank the constraints of another takes the separation of modules beyond the different strata posited in Lexical Phonology. Although the different modules in Lexical Phonology interacted in the lexicon, the strata were different and the rules operated in different ways with different results. OT has within itself the possibility of blurring the boundaries between the modules. This offers many advantages for the study of interface phenomena, since the theory is now free to allow for the interaction of the different modules. However, we should not lose the perspective of the extreme power of this freedom, and we need to be very careful not to confuse the issues further. Nevertheless, this new possibility opens the doors to analyzing language structure from a different perspective.

Among other contributions made by OT, one of the most relevant is the possibility to explain variation within languages and/or dialects and with it the possibility to explain all the possible forms in a language, while disallowing those that are not part of the system. Antilla and Cho (1998) show how we can explain language variation using the same mechanisms to explain Universal Grammar within OT. This opens a new way to study and explain variation and change in languages.

Traditional Generative Theory was limited to explaining only the correct forms, but it could not account for language variation without making reference to complete different grammars, that is, a form could be correct in one grammar but not well formed in another. There was no resource for different forms coexisting within the same grammar and no way of stating what forms were definitely not parts of any possible grammar of the language. In other words, it was impossible to identify the forms that would not be considered as part of a language by any of its speakers.

Antilla and Cho (1998) show that partial ordering works better than multiple grammars when trying to explain variation in language. They find that in Finnish, with a syllable-counting morphology, words with an even number of syllables are inflected differently from words with an odd number of syllables. This is a metrical phenomenon, and morphology reflects the alternation between stressed and unstressed syllables. According to Antilla and Cho, using a partial ordering within OT, we can come up with predictions on a weak theory of language change similar to the one postulated by Weinrich (1968, 99-100).

One of the most remarkable facts about language is that every native speaker recognizes every possible variety of his/her own language as different but at the same time recognizes both what belongs to his/her own language system and what is foreign. Part of the task of the linguist ought to include finding ways to explain this knowledge and its development. OT seems to have the methodological components needed to pursue this goal.

Within a notion of moraic theory, where moras are defined as the unit of quantity or weight for the syllable, Hubbard (1994) finds that moraic structure actually takes precedence over segmental factors in determining timing. Broselow, Chen, and Huffman (1997) do not confirm this strong claim, but they do seem to find that contrasts and differences in moraic association are reflected in segment duration patterns.

McCarthy and Prince (1993) stipulate that alignment at the edges of prosodic and morphological domains is behind a number of phonological and morphophonological processes. Previously, Selkirk (1986) had made reference to the interface between syntax and prosody, indicating that word edges have functional importance. It seems we need a constraint that demands correlation between the edges of the feet and the edge of the prosodic word.

One of the most recently discussed elements in OT is the amount, nature, and order of constraints. One of the major tenets of this theory is that all constraints are present in all languages: they are part of universal grammar. Differences between languages are therefore explained by different constraint ranking.

There are two major types of constraints within OT: 1) structural (well-formedness) and 2) faithfulness (matching input-output). We can say that type 1) constraints play a major role in language acquisition and change, while type 2) constraints tend to represent the ideal final state of acquisition, where the input and the output are exactly the same. Undoubtedly the nature of the variable ranking of these two types of constraints determines the actual form used in the language system.

Following is a list of the most common constraints that have been postulated in different OT studies. This list is by no means exhaustive, but it is included here as a guide and aid to further explain the topics at hand. This list can be used as an advanced organizer and as a point of reference for further reading.

List of Most Common OT Constraints

ONSET: "Every syllable has an Onset" (Prince and Smolensky, 1993; cited in Blevins, 1997).

*COMPLEX (no complex onsets) (Prince and Smolensky, 1993).

*COMPLEX-O (no complex onsets) (Levelt, Schiller, and Levelt, 2000).

*COMPLEX-C (no complex coda) (Levelt, Schiller, and Levelt, 2000).

ONSETSONORITY: For two segments to be parsed into the onset, they must observe the maximum distance in the sonority scale: the first one must belong to the set of least sonorous consonants, and the second one to the set of most sonorous consonants (Colina, 1995).

MAXI-O: Every input segment has a correspondent in the output (McCarthy and Prince, 1994).

BI (Base Identity): Given an input structure [X Y], output candidates are evaluated for how well they match [X] and [Y] if the latter occur as independent words (Kenstowicz, 1995).

UE (Uniform Exponence): Minimize the differences in the realization of a lexical item (morpheme, stem, affix, word) (Kenstowicz, 1995).

ALIGNLEFT: The left edge of every foot is aligned with the left edge of the prosodic word (McCarthy and Prince, 1993b, 1994).

PARSE-σ: Every syllable must belong to a foot (Prince and Smolensky, 1993).

FTBIN: Feet must be binary either at the moraic or syllabic level (Prince, 1980; McCarthy and Prince, 1986, 1993).

FOOT-FORM (TROCHAIC), Ft—s (s) s (w) (syllable strong, syllable weak, quantity insensitive foot (Hayes, 1991; Kager, 1992).

PARSE-SYLL: All syllables must be parsed by feet (Liberman and Prince, 1977; Halle and Vergnaud, 1987).

WEIGHT-TO-STRESS: Heavy syllables bear stress.

NONFINALITY: Similar to Extrametricality (Prince and Smolensky, 1993).

STRESS-FAITH: A stressed Input must have as its Output correspondent a stressed element (Pater, 1997). Similar to MAXFT-HEAD (Itō, Kitagawa, and Mester, 1996] and HEADMATCH (McCarthy, 1995).

ANCHOR-RIGHTI-O: There is correspondence between elements at the right edge of the Input word and the Output word (McCarthy and Prince, 1994, 1995).

I-CONTIG: The portion of the Input string standing in correspondence forms a contiguous string. Nonadjacent elements in the Input cannot become adjacent in the Output (McCarthy and Prince, 1995). If we make CONTIG relative to prosodic category like in Lamontagne (1996), we will have I-CONTIG-σ, which will require that the portion of the Input string standing in correspondence with the constituents of a syllable form a contiguous string; in other words, no skipping syllables.

Some Constraints According to the Sonority Scale

*V-ONS>>*L-ONS>>*N-ONS>>*F-ONS. Pater (1997) converts the two first ones (vowels and liquids) into *APROXIMANT-ONSET.

MORAICCODA: All coda consonants must be dominated by a mora (Broselow et al., 1997).

SYLLBIN: Syllable weight should not exceed two moras (Broselow et al., 1997).

NOSHAREDMORA: Moras should be linked to single segments (Broselow et al., 1997).

NOCMORA: The head of a mora must be a vowel (Broselow et al., 1997).

MORAFAITH: The number of moras linked to the input must be the same as the number of moras linked to the output. The constraint is violated if there is a mismatch (Broselow et al., 1997).

III.
Spanish Morphophonology and Language Acquisition

The Minimal Word in the Developmental Stages[1]

The phonetic shape of the minimal word in child language, imposing what appears to be a disyllabic maximum on word size at this learning stage, has been the subject of much discussion. This limit on word size begins at about age two. When children of this age attempt longer words, they truncate them to satisfy the two-syllable word limit. Regardless of the nature of this constraint, it disappears during language development and appears to play no role in adult language.

For English, it appears that we have a constraint to keep stressed and final syllables in children's truncation patterns attested by forms like [ɛlfʌn] 'elephant.' The fact that the final [t] does not appear in the truncated form gives us insight into the development of syllable structure: at this stage consonant clusters are not allowed in final position. The final rhyme is almost always selected in truncated forms, but sometimes the onset of the medial syllable is chosen over the one in the final syllable: [baki] for 'broccoli.' It seems that what determines choosing one onset over the other is which one is the less sonorous. If this is true, in the *mequica [mekika] for mecánica "mechanic" Spanish example analyzed below, we could argue that the child is choosing the [k] instead of the [n] following the sonority scale where obstruents are less sonorous than nasals.[2] This would be similar to what Pater (1997) claims for the truncated forms in English child language, but with not much consistency. In Spanish, the right edge foot is preserved in polysyllabic words. In López Ornat's (1994) corpus, the subject says *miámelos for míramelos "look at them on me" (or "for me"). In this utterance the subject is showing the operation of the Spanish three-syllable window for stress placement. Stress cannot appear in Spanish on the fourth syllable from the end and gets shifted to the antepenultimate syllable. This learner is not interpreting los as a stress-less clitic in this case. Compare *miámelo with *abóchame for abróchame. There is no stress shift in this case because the stress remains on the third syllable.

Even though we do not know exactly how speakers know when a word begins and ends, the fact that children seem to perceive better the beginning and endings of words is a clear indication that elements at the edges are salient. Pater (1997) considers that the elements that tend to be preserved are either heads of constituents or at the edges of domains. But we need to pay attention to what constituent is taken into consideration: the foot or the prosodic word. He also mentions the constraint STRESS-FAITH, to make sure the input and the output have the same stress, and the constraint ANCHOR-RIGHTI-O, to keep the right edges in correspondence.

If we observe the form 'maracas' in English, which is reported as [ma:kas] in truncated children speech, we cannot say exactly what vowel is truncated: the one in the first syllable or the stressed vowel. With the constraint of *A-ONS, we could say that it is the liquid in the second onset that is deleted, leaving the two vowels in contact. The OCP represented here as the constraint *REPEAT would eliminate one of the instances of this vowel. The same seems to apply for the English pronunciation of "garage" as [ga:dӡ] in child speech.

Looking at the English data, there seems to be a conflict between what are the most salient positions: the beginning and end or the stressed and end. What seems to be stable at all points is the Strong-Weak selection for the trochaic foot together with a required disyllabic word length. The pronunciation of [plis] for 'police' shows that MAXI-O has been promoted over *COMPLEX. Pater (1997) considers *pomus as the optimal candidate for the word 'hippopotamus' in child language in English, retaining the stressed and rightmost syllable. He bases this conclusion on the restriction on the phonetic shape of child language with a disyllabic maximum on word size. Beginning at age two, when children attempt to pronounce longer words, they are truncated to satisfy the word limit.

Echols and Newport (1992) assume that syllables are lost in children's speech due to misperception of the adult form, but Pater (1997) does not agree with this. It can be added that his is not only a question of misperception but of misproduction as well. The salience of particular constituents is responsible for the child's grammatical reproduction of what is heard.

Colina (1997) considers the OT account a better way to explain why two-word forms like [pub.lin.do] *pub lindo* "beautiful pub" do not re-syllabify into [pu.blin.do]. Within a rule formation approach, this would have been explained by not allowing re-syllabification to apply between words. Colina disregards this explanation as an ad-hoc way to explain away the lack of re-syllabification. Even though her treatment of these cases is quite accurate, the fact that re-syllabification is more restricted between words than within them is not necessarily ad-hoc, and it is actually quite enlightening: it refers exactly to the saliency of word edges. Colina uses an OT account to say that *CODA is irrelevant to explain [pub.lindo], but it is relevant to explain [ha.blar] *hablar* "to speak." This attempt at an explanation does not seem to be less ad-hoc than the one provided by the rule formation approach. If anything, the rule formation approach is more explanatory. All things being equal, it is always preferable to have the same processes explained by the same account. In any case, we can say that some speakers do make the re-syllabification in [pu.blindo], which will unify the previous accounts and show at the same time that the same processes apply in both contexts. Examples such as *pub lindo* show us that the speakers do have morphological information available when putting words together.

Kenstowicz (1995) offers the constraint *S]CODA, which dominates FAITH to ban [s] in a coda. Colina (1997) uses this constraint with no further formulation to explain the aspiration of [s] in the dialect of Granada in southern Spain. It is obvious that this constraint needs to be better formulated in order to provide a sensible explanation of the facts. As it stands, it provides nothing more than an ad-hoc resource: it tells us what happens and where, but not why. Although Colina's explanation may be descriptively correct, it fails to explain why [h] re-syllabification on the onset only happens in speakers that always aspirate the final [s] and who appear to be well on their way to eliminating final [s] completely. Speakers who only aspirate (not eliminate) on a regular basis, or have variation between [s] and [h] in coda position, do not have aspirated [h] in onset position. In dialects that always present aspiration, we also have instances of loss of the initial aspirated consonant. This does not happen in speakers who do not eliminate the final [s] altogether: [de.hecho], the pronunciation of *desecho* "piece of rubbish," by [s] aspirating speakers does not become [de.cho] for non-[s]-eliminating speakers. The differences encountered here are better explained with the constraints ONSET and NOCODA acting together. It is important to notice that even within an OT system, Colina needs to refer to morphological information indicating that phonology and morphology interact in these formations.

María, the subject in López-Ornat's study (1994), pronounces **hipo-cóntano* at 2 years, **popote* at 2 years one month, **pipótamo* at 2:03, and *hipopótamo*/hipopót*/hipopó* at 2:04 for the word *hipopótamo* 'hippopotamus.' The first attempt shows that the speaker, although already in control of tri-syllabic words, has problems with polysyllabic words like this one. First she breaks the word in two, but keeps the exact number of syllables. Noteworthy at this stage is the addition of *–n* in **hipo-cóntano* to help maintain the stress in the antepenultimate syllable. All the target vowels are in place, but the consonants show some non-target segments: *c* replaces *p,* and *n* replaces *m*.

Popote preserves the three middle syllables, but, not having a closed syllable on the antepenultimate, regularizes the stress on the penultimate. This utterance presents a very good example of knowledge of some mechanics of gender marking in Spanish at this early age. The target word is masculine ending in *–o,* but the child does not say ***popoto*.[3] The third syllable of the word pronounced is the manifestation of the syllable *-ta,* but although it violates a faithfulness constraint according to OT theory, the girl changes the *a* of *ta* for an *–e*. Uttering an *–a* would have made the form feminine: ***popota*.

*Pipótamo is almost target-like with the exception of the initial *–p* added to satisfy the ONSET constraint. Observe that the use of this *p* at the beginning of

the word prevents the realization of the second syllable *–po*. If it were included, we would have ended up with **pipopótamo. This form would have been excluded by the Obligatory Contour principle, which seems to restrict continuous similar onset consonants to two; three equal consonants (three *p*s) are not allowed.

The two truncation examples found in the pronunciation of these forms include everything from the beginning of the word to the stressed syllable, signaling the presence of an ALIGNLEFT constraint. *Hipopót maintains the *–t* in order to keep the stress in the last syllable; *hipopó retains the stress, but follows the *CODA constraint eliminating the voiceless consonant in coda position. Observe that we do not have examples of **pótamo, which would have signaled an ALIGNRIGHT constraint. This could have been another possible truncation keeping everything from the stressed syllable to the end of the word. The only possible explanation for the nonexistence of this form could be that the child language needs a closed syllable on the penult to place the stress there. This goes contrary to Fikkert (1994). According to this author, syllable quantity has not emerged at this stage, and therefore syllables, not moras, are counted. We have to look more in detail at a larger number of examples of children's data to see what process is operating here. What these two truncated forms seem to indicate is that the child has learned that the stress in Spanish needs to be closer to the right edge of the word, indicating what looks like a contradiction: the child is using ALIGNLEFT as the high-ranking constraint for word analysis, but ALIGNRIGHT as the higher-ranked constraint for stress assignment, mimicking what the established language system does: counting syllables left to right but assigning stress from right to left. This contradicts Hayes (1995), where the kind of foot required by a language morphological system is commonly the same as that required by its stress system.

In Pater (1997), the form *pomus is selected as the optimal candidate in child language for the word 'hippopotamus': in this example the rightmost and stressed syllables are preserved. No information is provided about why the syllable *-ta* is omitted. With MAXI-O, *-mus* will be unparsed and therefore not optimal. There seems to be a constraint for the preservation or perception in this case for the right side of the word, that is, for the end of the word to be preserved. With the constraints presented in Pater and with ALIGNLEFT, there is not an obvious explanation for this occurrence. The fact that what children produce is *pomus tells us what the optimal candidate would be, but it does not tell us why just yet. The child language represented here creates a binary foot with the stressed syllable and the syllable at the right edge of the word (the final syllable).

About *Palas Mequicas* and Other Things

As we have seen looking at the data from López Ornat (1994), at the beginning stages of native language learning we encounter the tendency to have a majority of two-syllable words and conservation of the beginning and end of the word. This will change later on to a stage where the endings of words are preserved.

In Spanish, one of our subjects in the language development stage produced *mequica* [mekíka] for *mecánica* [mekánika] "mechanic." It is obvious that this child's language development is now beyond the two-syllable stage, but it does not admit a word of more than three syllables yet. What is interesting about this output is that it is precisely the stressed syllable that gets deleted, with stress moved to the right as a result. It seems that this child still has a constraint about keeping stress on the penultimate syllable. Although we would expect that the syllable *ni* would be deleted, the *-i-* on that syllable is retained and only the *an* portion of the world is omitted. It is the Strong-Weak pattern at the right edge of the word that chooses the winning candidate, but the child still has a high ranking of both ALIGNLEFT and ALIGNRIGHT in order to preserve the beginning and the end of the word. In Table 3.1 we have a possible ranking of these facts.

Table 3.1. Possible Constraint Rankings for *mecánica* "mechanic" (fem.) (adj.)

Input: "mecánica"	ALIGN LEFT	ALIGN RIGHT	* 4 syl.	ST-P	FAITH-S
a. mecánica			*	*	
☞b. mequica					*
c. ánica	*		*	*	
d. anica	*				*
e. mecaní		*		*	*

The foot (*mecá*) violates this constraint with a Weak-Strong pattern. In child language, the first syllable of the foot invariably receives main stress, stress that reduces to secondary when encountering the last foot, which doesn't violate any of the aforementioned constraints.

The structure for the child in Spanish is closer to [(méca)(níca)]. With this pattern in mind, the second syllable of the first foot behaves just like the syllable *ni* in the adult language. The stress falls on *cá* in the adult language because the *nic* particle is not somehow attached to a foot and therefore is not stressed. As we will see later, the affix *–ic-* behaves as a non-carrier of stress in much the same way that terminal markers do.

Pater (1997) reports children English learners preserving the stressed and the last syllable in truncated forms, but he also refers to maintaining the initial ONSET and the last syllable. He explains this as a tendency to omit a liquid or a nasal like [ma:kas] '*maracas.*' We could say that together with a tendency to maintain the stressed and last syllables, there is also a tendency to keep the first onset and the last syllable, even when a stressed syllable has to disappear in the process. This becomes clearer with the examples from Spanish.

If what determines choosing one onset over another involves selecting which one is the less sonorous, in the **mequica* example we could argue that the child is choosing the [k] instead of the [n] following the sonority scale in which obstruents are less sonorous than nasals. This would be similar to what Pater (1997) claims for the truncated forms in English child language, a phenomenon that occurs without much consistency.

According to Slobin (1973), suffixes are learned before prefixes, since children pay more attention to the ends of words than to beginnings. This is possibly true at some point in the developmental stage, but forms like *pala *mequica*, as pronounced by our subject, can only be explained with a high ranking constraint maintaining the beginning of the word and the ending. Only in this way can we explain a non-target form that eliminates precisely the stressed vowel, which seems to be the most resilient segment in learning systems. In **mequica*, the first syllable *me-* has to be preserved as well as the last syllable following the conjunct constraint ALIGNLEFT/ALIGNRIGHT.

Notice also that this utterance gives us an example of how phrasal rhythm affects production at this stage. The target form *pala mecánica* "mechanical shovel" violates the stressed-unstressed pattern of syllables in Spanish. There is also a constraint to three-syllable words, which means that one of the middle syllables has to be eliminated in order to satisfy the constraint. Also, it looks like we have a constraint that restricts the placement of stress to the originally stressed vowel, which will prevent forms such as **meca from appearing. Notice that, according to this, **mecá would be possible.

Syllable Acquisition in L1

Bernhardt and Stoe-Gammon (1996) identified a group of expected characteristics of child phonology across languages which are of interest when compared to the Spanish data. We will refer here only to those characteristics that are pertinent to the data studied.

CV Syllables as Single Units or Binary Combinations CV.CV

In López Ornat's data we found examples of the following groups[4]:

V: **a**: **a**.mí, **a**.mir (*a dormir* "let's go to sleep"), **a**.pí (*a pintar* "let's paint"), **a** vé (*a ver* "let's see"), **a** (s) (las). *a* represents the preposition *a*.
   e: pa **e** ma (*papá y mamá*). The conjunction *y* "and," **e** mí (*es mío* "it's mine," **e** vestido (*el vestido* "the dress"); **e**.te (*este* "this one") (masc.) , **e**.ta (*esta,* "this one") (fem.).
   o: **o** ta (*dónde está* "where is it?"), **o** milo (*lo miro* "I look at it").
V.V: **í.a** *(mira* "look!"), **o.e** (*coche* "car"), **o.e** (*colores* "colors"), **e.e** (*vete* "go away!"), **í.o** (*tío* "uncle")
V.V.CV: **a.ú**.pa ("Up you go!" "Upsy Daisy")
V.CGV: **a**.gua, a.baa (*agua* "water")
VGV: **aio** (*adiós* "good bye")
V.GVC: a.ios (*adiós* "good bye")
V.GV: a.ió (*adiós* "good bye")
V.CGV.CV: a.mia.mo (?)
V.CV.CV: A.ca.ña (*Encarna*) (fem.) (proper noun)

V.CV.V.CV: a.pi.í.ta (*tapita* "small lid")
V.CV: a.pá (*tapar* "to cover")
VC.CV: An.ti (*Santi*) (short for Santiago)
CV.CV: ti.ta (*blanquita* "small white thing/person/animal") (fem.)
CV.CGV: ga-sia (*gracias* "thank you")
CGVG.CGVG: guau.guau (*guau, guau* "bow wuau")
CV.V: mí.a (*mira* "look!")

One of the most striking characteristics of Spanish is the constant and strong saliency of vowels in this language. We can see examples of this from the very first stages of language development: *coche* "car" is represented in the child's language by *o.e*. Observe the nonexistence of three-syllable words at this stage: *colores* is represented as *o.e*, not *o.o.e*. Note that this instance would also violate the *REPEAT constraint.

Onset Clusters Before Coda Clusters

Predictions for English with consonant codas play an important role in stress assignment. The only onset cluster we find in our data at the earliest stages is *st*, which, curiously enough, will not be a part of the learned Spanish inventory. The subject in López Ornat's study utters forms such as **no.sta* (*no está* "it's not here"), which coexists with **nos.ta* and **no.ta*; also **o.sta* (*dónde está* "where is it?"), which coexists with **os.tá*.

The first instance of an onset cluster representative of the Spanish learning inventory is in the word **flol, flor* "flower" at age 1:09. After this there are no instances of onset clusters until age 2:05, where we find **fio/frio, frío* "cold." From 3:06 on, we encounter more examples of consonant clusters, but only of the type consonant-liquid (*l, r*) and with inconsistent accuracy: we still find **paya* for *playa* "beach," **tozo* for *trozo* "a piece of," **tabajao* for *trabajado* "worked," **estopeao* for *estropeado* "spoiled," **ten* for *tren* "train," **atás* for *atrás* "behind," **mientas* for *mientras* "while," **gande* for *grande* "big," **caro* for *claro* "clear," etc.

Forms that deserve to be mentioned here are *Mardid/Madid* for *Madrid* and *marde/madre* for *madre* at 2:11, where *COMPLEXONSET is obviously ranked higher than *CODA and IO at this learning stage, leading to metathesis. An IO violation is preferred to the presence of a consonant cluster at the beginning of the syllable. It is interesting to see that the direction of the segment's movement is different in *Mardid* and *marde*. In both cases the *–r–* moves to the left of the target position. Interestingly, permeating this movement is the constraint about *COMPLEXCODAS, as moving the *r* in *Madrid* to the right would have meant the appearance of a complex coda: either **Madird* or **Madidr*.[5] In *madre*, moving the *r* to the right would have created a plausible form, but it seems that a coda in non word-final position is preferred to a coda in word final position.

Table 3.2. Possible Rankings for *Madrid* (proper name)

Input: "Madrid"	*COMPLEX-C	*COMPLEX-O	IO
a. Madrid		*!	
☞b. Mardid		*	*
c. Madird	*!		*
d. Madidr	*!		*
e. Madí			*! *!

We found no instances of coda clusters in this subject's data, which is what we should expect based on the complete Spanish learning system, where coda clusters are extremely rare and are only produced in forms coming from other languages. Levelt, Schiller, and Levelt (2000) say that Spanish allows complex onsets but no complex codas. They postulate the need to have some conjoined constraints like *COMPLEX-O, *COMPLEX-C, which would be ranked above two separate constraints, *COMPLEX-O and *COMPLEX-C, respectively. According to these authors, languages like Spanish require a ranking in which FAITH outranks *COMPLEX-O, but not *COMPLEX-C (2000, 262).

Early Specification of [+nasal]

All nasal segments are clearly present very early in this child's speech, as exemplified by forms such as *má* for *mano* "hand," *a mí* for *a dormir* "let's go to sleep," *mañá* for *mañana* "tomorrow," etc.

Appearance of (Less Complex) [-cons, +sonorant] Glides Before [+cons, +sonorant] Liquids

We find a perfect example of this in the utterance of *ties* for *tres* "three," where a semi-consonantal glide appears in place of the liquid *–r–*. The vibrant *–r–* appears very late in Spanish acquisition. By the end of López Ornat's recordings, her subject has yet to acquire full control of this segment. In some instances, we find a substitution of *–l–* for *–r–*, as in *blazo* for *brazo* "arm" and *liblo* for *libro* "book." We found only one instance of initial [R]: [RO.to] *roto* "broken," which is immediately replaced by [lo.to], and one instance of final [r] [mir], which is consistently deleted [mí]. We have not encountered any instances of internal [r] where we know there's a distinction in Spanish between [r] and [R].[6] We can make the assumption that at this point in the learning paradigm the child has only one [r], but we need to look further to confirm this idea. The late stage of acquisition of [r] in Spanish is clear in the inconsistencies in the pronunciation of this sound even at age 3:11, when all other segments are clearly established in the system of the child.

In terms of what consonants can appear in syllable final position, we have not seen [l], which is usually substituted with a final stressed vowel, as in the target word *mal*, represented by [má].

Crosslinguistically, Obstruents Are Less Likely to be Voiced in Word Final Position

This means that [+voice] in onsets would be more likely to be found before [+voice] in codas. Besides *n* and *l*, which appear very early in coda position, most other consonants in codas tend to either be voiceless or devoiced in that position. Generally in Spanish and in the speech of the subject studied here, coda consonants tend to devoice in final position. At this very early age, we already find an example of devoicing in final position in **parez* for *pared* "wall," which is a fairly common occurrence in adult speech as well. The voiced *r* also appears in coda position, but it is not fully acquired until quite late.

Default Place Feature Coronal [+anterior]

In Spanish, most consonants allowed to appear in coda position are specified as [+coronal] [+anterior], the only exceptions being *ch* and *s*, specified as [+coronal][-anterior]. Of these two, *ch* only appears in coda position in words of foreign origin. [s], on the other hand, appears freely in coda position both in internal final and absolute final position.

One of the characteristics of modern Spanish is the aspiration and/or deletion of *s* in final position. This process can be explained in two different ways or as a combination of both. Before venturing a conclusion, let us take a look at some background information.

Lleó, Prinz, El Mogharbel, and Maldonado (1996), in their longitudinal study of five children acquiring German in Hamburg and four children acquiring Spanish in Madrid, found that labials were the most frequent articulation place in Spanish babbling and in the word production for both languages. Their data includes information from 0-1:8 years old. This study fits nicely into this discussion because it ends at about the same age that López Ornat's study begins. In Lleó's study, velars are always higher for the Spanish group, as well as palatals. They found some interesting results about the fricative variants of [β, δ, γ]: while German children produced a much higher percentage of stops than fricative plus approximants, Spanish children produced a similar number of both groups. In order to see if the high numbers of fricatives and approximants in Spanish were somehow related to the spirantization process, they extracted all possible realizations of spirantization from the approximants and fricative group and found significant intergroup differences: the consonants [β, w, v, δ, γ] were significantly more frequent in two stages of the Spanish data.

They found even higher numbers of laryngeals in Spanish than German, even though according to them there are no laryngeals in Spanish, neither phonemically nor phonetically. They explain their numbers by saying that laryngeals are the least marked consonants in the feature geometry tree and are related to processes of debuccalization in different languages. One possible case of debuccalization is the process of [s] aspiration in Spanish, which has been explained as a process of delinking of the place features. If we could follow the idea of the laryngeals as the least specified consonant group, we could explain [s] aspiration with the same reasoning: emergence of the unmarked, which is what Morris (2000) does.

Lleó et al. (1996) state that consonants available for codas are almost exclusively coronals. Coda consonants are either coronal (liquids, nasals, and *s*) or assimilate to the point of articulation of the following obstruent. In the same study, closed syllables have a percentage of 2.4 in Spanish and 17.6 in German.

Table 3.3. includes a sample of the data extracted from López Ornat's study.

Table 3.3. Syllables with Coda

Child's Utterance		Target Form
Coda syllable final	Coda word final	
es.tas		*estas* "this ones" (fem.)
	mir	*dormir* "to sleep"
	ven	*ven* "you come"
is.ta		*esta* "this one" (fem.)
An.ti		short for *Santiago*
es.tas	es.tas	*estas* "these ones" (fem.)
nos.tá		*no está* "he/she/it is not here"
	Qui.tín	*Chiquitín* "little one" (masc.)
	a.sias	*gracias* "thank you"
om.be		*hombre* "man"
	a.pa.tos	*zapatos* "shoes"
	a.chús	onomatopoeic form for "sneezing"
aan.de		*grande* "big"
	me.dias	*medias* "socks/stockings"
	lo.lot	*dodot* "diaper"
	bis	*Luis* (proper name) (masc.)
es.te		*este* "this one" (masc.)
os.tá		*dónde está* "Where is it?
	Tas	onomatopoeic form
	Men	*ven* "you come"
	Tes	*tres* "three"
sus.to		*susto* "scare"
	Pes	*pies* "feet"
	Lus	*luz* "light"
ti(s)ta/tis.ta		*triste* "sad"[7]
tas.to		*trasto* "rubbish"
ton.to		*tonto* "dumb" (masc.)
es.tá		*está* "he/she/it is"

Table 3.4. Sample of Number of Syllables at One Year (cont'd.)

Age	One syllable		Two syllables		Three syllables		More
	V#	C#	V#	C#	V#	#C	
1:07	gue		te.ne				
	má						
	é		no.tá				
			a.guá				
			e.te				
			a.mí[8]				
	a						
		mir					
			no.sta				
	Aio[9]		aio?				
	Maa[10]		maa?				
	ma						
	pa						
			e.ta				
		ven					
			is.ta				
			a.sia		amiamo		
			ga.sia				
	pí		ma.ñá				
		Aios[11]		aios?			
				An.ti			
			Maia[12]		Maia?		
		tas					
	aió		es.te				
			ma.má				
				és.te			
			pa.pá				
		men					
			a.baa				
					apiíta		apiíta?
			a.pá				
			a.cá				
				a.sias			
				a.car			
			Po.quí				
	po						
	qué						
			pa.quí				
			poo.quée				
				os.tá			

Table 3.4. Sample of Number of Syllables at One Year (cont'd.)

Age	One syllable		Two syllables		Three syllables		More
	V#	C#	V#	C#	V#	#C	
	miau						
		tes					
		pés					
			o.stá				
			nos.tá				
			mí.a				
			í.a				
			o.e				
			co.te				
			a.ti				
				om.be			
							a.ma.di.llo
			ve.ye				
			ti.ta		e.ti.ta		
			a.pá				
			a.pa				
1:08			n.otá				
			qui.tín				
			aan.de				
			a.quí				
	tá						
	tó						
			o.sé				
			so.so				
			ca.na				
			no.tá				
			os.tá				
	buá				a.pa.tos		
			po.co				
			a.cá				
			es.te				
			si.lla				
			o.to				
			o.ta				
			ca.chá				
			e.e				
			co.llá - to.to				
1:07			bua.buá				
			guau.gua				

Table 3.4. Sample of Number of Syllables at One Year (cont'd.)

Age	One syllable		Two syllables		Three syllables		More
	V#	C#	V#	C#	V#	#C	
			u				
1:09			su.to				
				sus.to			
			í.to				
			a.bua				
				tas.to			
	mé		me.e				
	má		o.tá				
			a. ba				
			ti(s)ta/ tis.ta				
			ya.stá				
	ya		e.tá				
		lus					
	a		ti.sú		a.chús		
					es.tá		
					ton.to		
	meia						
	maia		me.dia		me.dias		
					es.tas		
					lo.lot		
			ro.to				
	aió?		ai.ó?				
			bo.llo				
			co.llo				

We can observe that only *a, e,* and *o* appear as the vowels in absolute final position. Instances of *i* and *u* appear at this stage in final position only accompanied by a consonant, either *n* or *s*, or are stressed in that position.

Notice the few instances of three-syllable words, the almost complete absence of words of more than three syllables (there is only one four-syllable word), and the early appearance of glides, both pre-vocalic and post-vocalic, with a small preponderance of pre-vocalic glides.

Table 3.5. Syllable Structure: Consonants

Word initial	Word final	Syllable initial Word internal	Syllable final	Second in C cluster
b		b		
D[13]			d	
f				
g		g	g	
j [x][14]			j(x)	
[k](c, qu)		[k](c,qu)	l	
l		m	m	
m				
n	N[15]	n	n	
Ñ[16]		ñ		
p		p	p	
R.[17]				
	R		R[18]	
s	s	S[19]	s	
t	T[20]	t		
y				
	Z[21]		z	

A Brief Look at Consonants in Coda Position

Within the context of Optimality Theory, several constraints have been stipulated to reflect general processes of Universal Grammar. This section will study in some detail what processes affect consonants in coda position in Spanish. In order to do this, the following constraints will be examined:

ONSET: syllables must have onsets.

*CODA: syllables must not have a coda.

*COMPLEX-O: no complex onsets in syllables.

*COMPLEX-C: no complex codas in syllables.

According to Colina (1997), what she calls the onset rule applies both lexically and post-lexically or word-internally and across words, as exemplified by *las alas* "wings," resyllabified as [la.sa.las]. The complex onset rule only applies word-internally, but not between words: *pub lindo* "beautiful pub" is syllabified as [pub.lin.do] and not as [pu.blin.do]. Re-syllabification, or linking in Spanish, is explained by an ONSET constraint, according to which optimal syllables must have onsets.

The variety of Spanish studied more closely in the following section will be Andalusian Spanish, but other varieties will also be examined in order to achieve more explanatory adequacy.[22]

Consonants in Coda Position in Andalusian Spanish

Standard Spanish has a limited number of consonants that can appear in coda position in word-internal and absolute final position: They all happen to be coronal consonants: *t, d, z, s, n, l, r, rr*. The only one of the coronal consonants that does not appear regularly in absolute final position in Spanish is *ch*. The only peculiarity presented by this segment is that it is specified as [+coronal, -anterior]. All other consonants in this group, with the sole other exception of [s], are specified as [+coronal, +anterior].

Table 3.6. Consonants in Coda Position in Andalusion Spanish

S		
a. Disappears without leaving anything behind. [lo] *los* "them" (masc.)	b. Disappears changing the preceding vowel. [košíno] *cochinos* "pigs"	c. Disappears with gemination of the following consonant. [pattoría] *pastoría*
d. Disappears with aspiration. [doh] *dos* "two"	e. Remains in front of a vowel becoming part of the ONSET. [e.su.na] *es una* "it's one"	
R		
a. No change in word-internal position. [la:rgo] *largo* "long"	b. Disappears in absolute final position. [po] *por* "by, through"	c. Remains with change. [poR] *por* "by, through"
N		
a. Disappears in word final position. [swerta] *sueltan* "they release"	b. Remains with assimilation to the following consonant. [kwan.do] *cuando* "when"	c. Remains as alveolar in ONSET position. [Ko.nu.na] *con una* "with one" (fem.)
d. Reduces in final position. [matan] *matan* "they kill"		
L		
a. Disappears. [e] *el* "the" [l-arβo] *el árbol* "the tree"	b. Changes to r. [bwerβan] *vuelvan* "You (pl.) come back"	c. Remains. [el βerano] *el verano* "summer"

It is generally agreed that the universal optimal syllable is the one that fits the CV template. In Spanish, in particular, we can see that the processes occurring in coda position are signs of adjustments the language makes to fit the CV pattern, i.e., a limited number of consonants allowed to appear in coda position, the requirements for homorganicity in that position, the movement to onset position whenever this position is vacant, etc.

Prieto (1992) considers uncontroversial the fact that consonants in the coda do not count for a weight unit in Spanish, that is, there are no coda consonants considered to be moras. It is easy to agree with this for those consonants, such as *n* or *s*, that are expressions of a particular morpheme (i.e., a form of a terminal marker). Those word final coda consonants that do not represent a specific morpheme do tend to have weight attached to them and therefore could work as a mora. One example of this would be the fact that coda final consonants attract stress to the last syllable.

We can see an example of *s* re-syllabification in the utterances *soso* for *el oso/los osos* "the bear/the bears" in the subject in López Ornat's study.

Table 3.7. Possible Rankings for *los osos* "bears"

Input: "los osos"	ONSET	*CODA	2-SYLL	ONE-W	IO
a. lo.so.sos		*!*	*	*
b. o.sos	*!	*			
c. o.so.so		*		*	
d. lo.so				*	***
☞ e. so.so					***

The optimal candidate at this stage is the one that follows the pattern CV.CV in Table 3.7, has two syllables, and represents only one word. It is interesting to see that (d) has all of these characteristics but is not the optimal candidate because it keeps an element belonging to a different word.

The Awkward Status of –*n* in Final Position

The status of syllable or word final [n] in Spanish shows a kind of schizophrenic behavior. In Spanish we find linking of final [n] to a vowel in the following word. For example, *canción* "song" is syllabified as *can/ción*, and *elegante* "elegant" is syllabified as *e/le/gan/te*, but when we put these two words together in a phrase, we find they are re-syllabified as *can/ció/ne/le/gan/te*, where the final [n] is now the onset of a newly formed syllable. This onset [n] is pronounced as the unmarked alveolar [n], although it could have been pronounced as a velar in final position. Two things are clear in this re-syllabification process:

1. No attention is paid to whatever rule applied to [n] in final position (an [n] will be alveolar in initial position, regardless of any previous rule).

2. No constraints seem to be restraining this re-syllabification process. It is a fairly common and exceptionless process at the phrase level in standard Spanish. It is also common in inflection processes; i.e., *pan* "bread" can be pronounced with a final velar consonant, but when the plural marker [s] is added to it, we end up with *pa/nes* with an alveolar [n] in initial position, not a velar [ŋ]. We can say that when stress-shifting affixes are attached, the *n* in final position cannot be re-syllabified as an alveolar that begins the next syllable,

while when non-stressed shifting affixes are applied, the *n* re-syllabifies without any difficulty.

Harris (1983) stipulates that "velarized *n* and aspirated *s* occur in syllable-initial position only if they are also in word-final position and followed by a word that begins in a vowel, i.e., precisely the environment for Re-syllabification" (47). These examples are variable rules, as they do not necessarily apply in every situation.

It is also necessary to look at what happens to the final position [n] in other derivation examples. When the diminutive suffix is added to a word with a final [n], we have an extension added, and the final form for the diminutive of *pantalón* "pants" is not **pantalonito*, but *pantaloncito* instead. It is worth noting that in the Canary Islands we find examples of *pantalonito*. In these cases there seems to be a constraint against re-syllabification of final *n*.

In Spanish we also have examples like *llorón* "male person given to weeping," *lloroncito* "small male person given to weeping," and the feminine counterparts *llorona–lloroncita*. The first example is straightforward, but we would expect the second one to follow the pattern of vowel ending words as *casa* "house," *casita* "small house," *ventana* "window," *ventanita* "small window," but this is clearly not the case. It seems that the fact that *llorón* and *llorona* are derived words based on the suffix [-ón] is affecting the outcome of these forms.[23]

Bakovic (2000) denies the existence of a velar final in Spanish. He follows Trigo (1988) in arguing that the velar reported in certain varieties is nothing more than a debuccalized nasal represented as [N]. We could say that there is no velar [ŋ] in onsets in Spanish because [ŋ] is not a phoneme in Spanish, and only recognized phonemes in a language can appear in onset position. This is one possible way to explain the presence in Galician of velar *n* in syllable-initial position in examples with *un*, the masculine indefinite article. In Galician, *un* is pronounced with a velar *n* in final position, while the feminine indefinite article written as *unha* is pronounced with a velar *n* in syllable-initial position. This has given basis to the postulation of a phonemic velar *n* for Galician: a phoneme with very limited occurrence. It is of interest to mention that when forming the diminutives of words ending in *n* in Galician, we have the same increment as in Spanish, i.e., *Juan* "John," *Juanito/Juancito, Xoan–Xoanciño*.

Table 3.8. Possible Rankings for *algún* "some" (masc.)

algún[24]	ONSET	CODA-COR/ANT	*CMORA	*CODA
a. al.gúŋ		*		*
b. al.gu. ŋ			*	*
☞ c. al.gún				*

Bakovic considers that there is no velar *n* in coda final position in Spanish. He explains the nasal segment in that position as an example of debuccalization. A velar nasal in coda position in Spanish would be prevented from appearing by a restriction on the specification of [+coronal, +anterior] for all coda consonants in Spanish. Velar *n* is [-anterior] and as such is prevented from appearing in coda final position. Candidate (b) in Table 3.8 is not the optimal candidate because a consonant cannot be the nucleus of the syllable in Spanish, and (c) emerges as the winning candidate.

Table 3.9. Possible Rankings for *algunha* "some" (fem.) (Galician)

al.gúŋ+fem.	ONSET	*CMORA	*CODA	IO
a. al.gú.ŋ.a	*	*		
b. al.gúŋ.a	*		*	
☞c. al.gú.ŋa				
d. al.gú.na				*

The Galician facts can be explained by a lifting of the restriction of velar *n* in coda position. This creates the environment for re-syllabification to the beginning of the next syllable. This re-syllabification takes place in Galician at the word level. At the syntactic level this restructuring is not available.

Table 3.10. Possible Rankings for *alguna* "some" (fem.) (Spanish)

al.gún+fem	IO	CODA-COR/ANT	ONSET	*CODA
a. al.gúŋ.a	*	*	*	*
b. al.gú. ŋa	*			
☞c. al.gú.na				

While in Galician ONSET is ranked higher, in Spanish, IO has a higher ranking than ONSET, therefore the winning candidate for Spanish in Table 3.10 is (c).

Notes

1. The data used here for Spanish L1 acquisition comes from López Ornat Fernández, Gallo, and Mariscal (1994), who recorded a longitudinal corpus of child talk from a Spanish girl from the age of 1 year and 7 months to the age of 3 years and 11 months. The database studied has a total of 662 track entries, stopping at the age of 3:11. After track 648, which corresponds to age 3:10, all forms are target productions, so variation in syllable production stopped. It seems that at this point the girl had acquired all possible syllable combinations in Spanish. When pertinent for expository reasons, we also refer to our own observational data collected over the years from subjects in the language developmental stage.

2. From now on, non-target forms will be represented in italics with an asterisk, while target forms will be represented with italics. English glosses of Spanish forms will be written in quotes. English words referring to examples in English will be written using single quotes.

3. From now on, hypothetical forms that are never actually produced will be represented with two asterisks.

4. V stands for vowel, G stands for glide (either pre-vocalic or pos-tvocalic), and C stands for consonant. Syllable breaks are represented with a period (.), i.e. the word *casa* "house" has two syllables and would fit the description CV.CV indicating that the first syllable has a consonant as the ONSET, or beginning, and a vowel as the rhyme, or the end. This pattern is repeated in the second syllable.

5. It seems like metathesis is only allowed to skip a segment. If this is the case, this form would be even more implausible.

6. We use [R] here to represent the trill as in *carro* "car" [ka.Ro], different from *caro* "expensive" [ca.ro].

7. It is interesting to notice the introduction of –*a* as a feminine gender marker in the child's production. The target form *triste* "sad" has –*e* as the final word marker

8. Even though this word is pronounced as one word with two syllables, it is the representation of two words, *a dormir* "let's go to sleep."

9. It is not clear if this word is monosyllabic or bisillabic.

10. We do not know if this word is pronounced *ma.a or *maa.

11. Another form where it is not clear if we have a one-syllable word or a two-syllable word.

12. Again, we cannot tell how many syllables exactly.

13. In our data, [d] does not appear in the beginning of a word until 1 year 10 months in the word **didito/dedito* "small finger," and it does not appear again until 2 years 1 month in *disce* for *dice* "he/she says." This is something that needs to be investigated further.

14. *jobetes juguetes "toys": first instance at 1 year 11 months.

15. First instance at 1 year 10 months in *Manian for *Marian*.

16. We find it in only one instance: *ñeque.

17. *reló reloj "watch": first instance at 1 year 11 months.

18. *acar: appears as infinitive marker

19. It also occurs in syllable initial as the first element in a consonant cluster with *t*, only in instances of the verb *está*: **no.stá*. "he/she/it is not (here)."

20. *lolot for *dodot* "diaper." This is the only instance in the whole text.

21. The first instance occurs at 1 year 10 months in *parez for *pared* "wall."

22. The data from the Andalusian variety comes from *Textos andaluces en transcripción fonética*, a study done by Manuel Alvar, Antonio Llorente, and Gregorio Salvador, edited in 1995 by Manuel Alvar and Pilar García Mouton.

23. See chapter VII on diminutives for more information.

24. Although there is an ONSET violation on the first syllable of these forms, we are only looking at this time at the syllable with *n* in final position.

IV.
Stress and Intonation

Observations about Stress Assignment

Generally, the norm in Spanish when adding suffixes to words is to move the stress from its original position to the suffix. This is a consequence of the process by which Spanish adds suffixes to create new words. Suffixes in Spanish add either one or two syllables to the base to which they are attached. Aside from instances of what can be called ∅ suffixation, as in *el canto* "singing," *el habla* "speech, language," *el baile* "the dance," etc., that keep the stress in the original base, most suffixes in Spanish move the stress to the suffix. This was explained in generative phonology within the concept of the cycle. According to this notion, stress placement in Spanish is applied cyclically, which means that stress assignment rules applied again every time a suffix was added to a word: *cantar* to sing," *cantante* "singer," *canción* "song," *cancionero* "song book."

One very noticeable exception to the previous observations is the addition of the morpheme *–ic* to form adjectives: *magnífico* "magnificent, excellent," *práctico* "practical" (different from *practico* "I practice"), *estético* "esthetic." In these cases the stress is placed invariably on the syllable before the suffix. This has been explained as a case of extra-metricality (Harris, 1983). Elements at the edge of constituents can be lexically stipulated as being invisible to certain operations, in this case stress placement. The notion of extra-metricality is a useful tool to describe situations like this. It is obvious that the addition of suffixes like *-ic* does not affect the stress of the new word in the same way other suffixes do. It would be easy to be able to say that when this particular suffix is added, the stress remains on the original vowel. This seems to the case in forms such as *anestesia* "anesthesia," *anestésico* "anesthetic," *metro* "meter," *métrico* "metrical," *tono* "tone," *tónico* "tonic." But we only need to look at words like *anatomía* "anatomy," *anatómico* "anatomic," *órgano* "organ," *orgánico* "organic," *teléfono* "telephone," *telefónico* "telephonic," *átomo* "atom," *atómico* "atomic," etc. to see that the stress does not remain in the original vowel all the time. If we onsider *anatomía* as a derived structure with the form [[[an]atom]ía], where the base is [atom], the same as in the word *átomo,* we can then unite all these forms with the observation that the stress remains on the original vowel, unless keeping the stress in that position would violate the three-syllable window, which does not allow the stress to be placed farther back than the third syllable from the end of the word. This constraint explains all the cases where the stress is not on the original vowel.

So far we have described the case of a suffix which does not behave like other suffixes in Spanish, but we have not explained why this is so. We can resort to the history of the language and say that these forms are patterned after the original Latin stress, and therefore conclude that they are diachronic remnants, which cannot be explained in any other way from a synchronic standpoint. This is true up to a point. One thing we have not mentioned yet is the fact that the suffix *–ic* behaves exactly like terminal elements in Spanish regarding placement of stress: they do not affect it.

Spanish has been described as a three-syllable window language in relation to stress assignment. This means that stress cannot surface in Spanish farther back than the third syllable counting from the end of the word. The only two cases where stress seems to appear beyond the third syllable are adverbs in *–mente*: *prácticamente* "in a practical way, practically," and verb forms with clitics attached: *dándomelo* "giving it (masc.) to me."

In adverbs in *–mente*, the Real Academia stipulates that a written accent mark must be placed on the originally stressed syllable if the original form was proparoxitone and therefore had a written accent mark. Although these forms appear to be stressed on a syllable beyond the antepenultimate, in close examination we can see that in the adverb formation we have an example of a word level morphological process: *–mente* is added to the word *práctica,* and both parts keep the original stress. Notice that these adverbial forms are derived from the feminine of the original word, as the terminal feminine marker *–a* remains as part of the new word. The meaning of the new adverbial form in Spanish is *en (de) una manera práctica* "in a practical way," where the adjective *práctica* "practical," marked as feminine, agrees in gender and number with the noun it modifies. In this case the gender is feminine, and that is the reason why we have an *–a* in all vowel ending forms of this type of adverb.

In *dándomelo* "giving it (masc.) to me," the original verb form is *dando* "giving" and *me* "to me" and *lo* "it (masc.)" are the clitic forms of Spanish direct object pronouns, which are attached to the end of infinitives and present participles in Spanish. These clitics are supposed to be unstressed, although we are seeing a new development in the stressed nature of these forms. More and more we are hearing instances of verb plus clitic pronounced something like *dámeló* "give it (masc) to me," where the position of the clitic is emphasized by what looks like a type of pitch accent.

Besides the previous cases, stress in Spanish never fails to surface in one of the last three syllables of the word. We have forms like *sábana* "bed sheet," *sabana* "prairie," and *maná* "manna, godsend," where stress is clearly lexical.

There is no way we can predict stress placement based on the structure of the previous words. That said, there are a number of patterns that Spanish words seem to follow when assigning stress.

1. Words that end in a vowel tend to carry the stress on the penultimate syllable: *casa* "house," *mesa* "table," *mano* "hand," *pollo* "chicken," *repollo* "cabbage," *cuaderno* "notebook." A good number of Spanish words follow this pattern, as penultimate stress is somehow considered the most common of Spanish stress types.

The Real Academia de la Lengua, when establishing orthographic norms for the written language, decided to add to this generalization the consonants –*n* and –*s* because these consonants represent the plural morpheme (*s*), the morpheme for second person singular and plural in verbs (*s*), and the third person plural morpheme in verbs (*n*). These morphemes, being terminal elements, do not affect stress placement, but give us a large number of words ending in these consonants. Although the decision to include these consonants together with the vowels seems to be a good one, it creates some problems. Words ending in an –*n* that does not function as a word marker (plural or person and number morpheme) invariably place the stress on the last syllable. Unfortunately, because of the decision to include *n* and *s* with the vowels when assigning stress, we are left with an enormous number of words requiring a written accent. Although this is a mark of exception in Spanish, they are absolutely regular. Without exception, native speakers place the stress on the last syllable of words ending in *n*: *camión* "truck," *pantalón* "pants," *situación* "situation," etc. We only have to remember that before news on television became a part of daily life, people used to see the English word *Washington* written in newspapers, invariably pronounced it as *[gwasintón]*. This did not happen with the word *London* because it was almost without exception always translated to *Londres*.

The inclusion of –*n* and –*s* with the vowels does a good job of recognizing their function as word markers, which as such, do not affect stress placement. Unfortunately, this inclusion fails to recognize the status of final –*n* when it does not represent a word marker and complicates things unnecessarily. L1 and L2 teachers have to remind students not to write a written accent mark when these –*n* final words become plural: *camión* (sing.), but *camiones* (pl.).

There are a number of exceptions to the previous generalization for vowel-ending words: *café* "coffee," *papá* "dad, father," *Perú* "Peru," *rubí* "ruby." It is interesting to mention that these vowels that carry stress when in absolute final position tend to remain as part of the derivational base when suffixes are attached to create new words: *café–cafetera* "coffee maker," *cafetería* "cafeteria," *cafetal* "coffee plantation," *cafetalero* "related to coffee" (adj.), *cafecito* "small coffee," *cafés* "coffees." Compare this with words ending in non-stressed vowels such as *casa–casas* "houses," but *caserío* "small village," *casero* "landlord," *casita* "small house," *caserón* "big house, mansion," *casón* "big house." These facts tend to indicate the existence of a base structure of the type [cas]a] for *casa* and [café] for *café*. If this could be generalized for all similar forms, we could affirm that the level for stress placement in Spanish is the derivational base, not the root, and that stress falls on the last vowel of the derivational base. The only exceptions to this pattern would be proparoxytones such as *sábado* "Saturday" and *sábana* "bed sheet," unless we want to posit derivational bases such as [sab]ad]o] or [sab]an]a], which would place the stress on the *–a–* of the hypothetical root, and consider the second *–a–* as extrametrical, that is, non-visible for stress placement.

Words ending in *–e* present special problems. If the final vowel is stressed, they tend to behave as *café* above. But a good number of *–e* final words have penultimate stress: *padre* "father," *madre* "mother," *estudiante* "student," *almirante* "admiral," etc. *Padre* and *madre* keep the final *–e* when adding the diminutive: *padrecito, madrecita* (compare *compadrito* "dear godfather (from the point of view of the parent or godmother)" and *comadrita* "dear godmother").[1] The words *padrino* "godfather" and *madrina* "godmother," although related, are no longer considered to be diminutives of *padre* and *madre* and should therefore be considered as individual lexical entries.

The final *–e* in *almirante* "admiral" and *estudiante* "student" behaves like a terminal element. Although it does not give us clear information about gender (we need to find that information from the article *el estudiante* [masc.], *la estudiante* [fem.]), it disappears when adding new suffixes: *estudiantado* "student body," *almirantazgo* "admiralty."

2. Words that end in a consonant tend to have the stress on the last syllable. This group includes words with coda consonants such as *t, z, n, d, r, l, j*, etc.: *pared* "wall," *reloj* "watch," *canción* "song," *leer* "to read," *Aranjuez* (proper name), *verdad* "truth," etc.

3. Words that carry the stress on the third syllable from the end are called proparoxytones, and there is no special paradigm for these words, other than the fact that some of them follow the Latin stress pattern: 1) If the penultimate and the ultimate syllables are open, stress can fall on the antepenultimate: *Sábado* "Saturday," but compare *análisis* "analysis," which can be explained as an example of extrametrical final *s* in Latin. 2) Stress can fall on the antepenultimate if this syllable is a closed syllable: *carámbano* "icicle."

L2 Learning of Stress Placement in Spanish

In order to ascertain to what extent first-year L2 learners of Spanish were able to identify the stressed syllable, a study was conducted where students of first-year Spanish and L1 Spanish speakers were asked to identify the stressed syllable on nonce (made up) words. These words were designed to incorporate all possible syllable configurations and to include words from one to four or more syllables. The L2 Spanish learners were also asked to identify the stressed syllable in nonce forms resembling English words to see if they were transferring the English pattern into Spanish or actually acquiring a new parameter. The nonce forms were divided in two groups: one group was designated as Spanish forms only and one group as English forms only. Although there were different forms on both groups, there were a number of common words. When tabulating the data, the groups were divided into: 1) Nonce Spanish forms, 2) Nonce English forms, and 3) Nonce common forms. Group 2 was tabulated only for English L1 speakers, and Group 3 was tabulated for English L1 speakers as both English forms and Spanish forms, and for Spanish L1 speakers.

The following table presents a summary of the results. As before, C stands for Consonant, V for Vowel.

Table 4.1. Acquisition of Stress in L2

		Spanish L2 Learners % of responses				Spanish Natives % of responses		
Number of syllables		4+	3	2	1	3	2	1
Nonce Spanish forms								
1. CVCV				<u>70</u>	30		<u>93</u>	7
2. CVV (ie)				<u>58</u>	42		20	<u>80</u>
3. CVV (ia)				<u>79</u>	21		<u>100</u>	0
4. CVCVCV			40	<u>54</u>	5	20	<u>80</u>	0
5. CVCCVCCV			23	<u>67</u>	10	7	<u>93</u>	0
6. CVCVVCCVCV		19	28	<u>48</u>	5	17	<u>83</u>	0
7. CVCVC		1	7	34	<u>58</u>		10	<u>90</u>
Nonce English form								
8. CVCVCVCVCVC		9	<u>54</u>	28	9			
9. CVCVCVVCV		3	20	<u>59</u>	19			
10. CVCVCCVC			33	<u>51</u>	16			
11. CVCCVCVVC (ier)			16	17	<u>67</u>			
Nonce common forms								
12. CVCVC(s)	English			<u>89</u>	11			
	Spanish			<u>79</u>	21		<u>100</u>	
13. CVCCCVC(n)	English			<u>78</u>	22			
	Spanish			16	<u>84</u>		<u>100</u>	
14. CVCVCCV	English		41	<u>47</u>	12			
	Spanish		21	<u>63</u>	16		<u>100</u>	
15. CVCVCCVC(n)	English		12	<u>82</u>	6			
	Spanish		11	<u>47</u>	42			<u>100</u>
16. VCCVCVC(n)	English		28	28	<u>44</u>			
	Spanish			47	<u>53</u>		40	<u>60</u>
17. CVVCVCCV	English		<u>33</u>	<u>33</u>	<u>33</u>			
	Spanish	16	32	<u>47</u>	5	40	<u>60</u>	
18. CVCVCVVC(n)	English		18	<u>76</u>	6			
	Spanish		28	33	<u>39</u>			<u>100</u>

In Table 4.1 we can see that Spanish L2 learners have not yet acquired the Spanish stress system but have made some movements towards its acquisition. Although their percentages for selecting a particular syllable for stress are not as high as the ones selected by the native speakers, they tend to select the same syllable the native speakers do as the most likely to receive stress.

In general, native Spanish speakers tend to show more agreement in choosing the stressed syllable when looking at nonce words. L2 Spanish students show a wider degree of variation when choosing stressed syllables in both English and Spanish.

Taking into consideration that these are students in first-year Spanish, we can say that they are becoming aware of the Spanish stress system, although most of these students have not received explicit information on stress assignment in Spanish. Although stress and intonation do not receive a great deal of attention in beginning classes, the availability of input in the target language seems to be providing students with the necessary tools to acquire them.

Within the L1 system, intonation and stress are acquired rather early, occasionally before the talking stage.

Differences in Intonation:
An Example from Castilian and Galician Spanish[2]

In the previous section we mentioned that intonation and stress assignment are acquired quite early in the language learning stages. In this section, we will look at Spanish in contact with Galician to see what effect languages in contact have in the development of intonation systems.

The variety of Spanish spoken in Galicia has a special intonation pattern that makes it stand out within the Spanish-speaking communities. A common anecdotal reference refers to the singing quality of Galician speech. In this section, we will analyze how this pattern internal to Galician transfers to the Spanish spoken in the area. Speakers of Galician Spanish have a special intonation characterized by a perceived higher intensity of stressed syllables when compared to standard Spanish. Galician Spanish seems to have a special utterance final pitch accent.

The findings of this study corroborate impressionistic comments made by both Spanish and English speakers, all students in a Dialectology class at a major U.S. university who, while listening to a tape of a monolingual Galician speaker, all agreed with the perception that this particular speaker did not want to be interrupted. It was their impression that this speaker wanted to keep the floor for herself, as her utterances did not have the expected falling tone at the end.[3]

The data used for this study comes from tape recordings of Galician speakers made by the researchers of the Instituto da Lingua Galega as part of the data gathering process to prepare the *AGAL (ATLAS Lingüistico Galego)*[4] and from tape recordings of bilingual Spanish and Galician speakers, monolingual speakers of Spanish from Galicia, and monolingual speakers of Spanish from other areas of the Spanish-speaking world made by the author in Galicia and the United States. The data from the Instituto is all in Galician, with a majority of monolingual speakers in that language, and have the form of narratives told by individual informants. The Instituto compiled recordings from all the major areas where the language is spoken. For this study the tapes found to be more representative of the different areas were selected. Most of the data selected comes from South Western Galician coastal zones, specifically the Pontevedra area. The data recorded by the author is in the shape of unrehearsed conversations among the informants.

Electronic sound files were created from these tapes and run through a speech analysis tool to obtain spectrograms and diagrams for pitch, intensity, and frequency.[5] Since the data examined was not produced in a laboratory setting, but in actual conversations between native speakers, this study will contribute to the analysis of uninterrupted speech flow providing information about realistic rising and falling contours in actual samples of natural discourse.

Background Information

In the general literature, the term "pitch accent" has been used in different ways. Pierrehumbert (1980) defined it as a special lexical contrast in intonational tonal contours related to stress. Establishing the difference between stress, tone, and accent is not an easy task. Pitch has been identified as being the primary acoustic equivalent of tone and the perceptual signal of stress (Hyman, 1978). Nevertheless, the term "pitch accent" has been used to identify a third group of languages different from tone languages and stress-accent languages. In tone languages, pitch distinguishes items lexically, whereas in stress-accent languages, pitch is non-distinctive. In tone languages, the pitch of each syllable is unpredictable, and syllables, having no identifiable prominence, must be marked in the lexicon for tone. In stress-accent languages, such as English, the accented syllable is more prominent, and therefore the melody of the word can be predicted based on that prominence. Chinese and Thai are typical examples of tonal languages. In the so-called pitch-accent languages, placement of accent determines what syllable is going to have more prominence. Japanese has been mentioned as a proto-typical pitch-accent language, based on the fact that we find a three-way distinction between High Low, Low High, and unaccented words.

Hasegawa (1999) studies the Japanese Tokyo dialect and finds that vowels devoice, regardless of their accented status. Hasegawa considers that prominence does not guarantee permanence of the vowel in Japanese and therefore concludes that there is no connection between prominence and accented status in Japanese. In her opinion, Japanese should be treated as a tone language and not as a stress-accent language, in spite of the fact that tones do not necessarily follow the expected pattern and do not have—and least in the Tokyo dialect— the same prevalence in the surface structure. She uses this finding to claim that Japanese should be studied as a tone language and not as a stress-accent language, therefore giving basis for a three-way distinction in Japanese.

In English a prominent syllable is usually maintained; that is, it is not reduced. Galician and Spanish tend to group themselves with English in this aspect, with no reduction of prominent or accented vowels. We find a distinction between Galician and English, on one side, and Spanish, on the other, in the treatment of accented vowels versus non-accented ones. In Galician in particular we find examples of reduction and sometimes even deletion of unaccented vowels, i.e., *A Coruña* → *A Curuña* → *A Cruña* "La Coruña." In Spanish, we find a slight reduction of unstressed vowels, but this reduction is not significant, and it does not alter the quality of the original vowel.[6] We can hypothesize that in Galician, prominence and accent do go hand in hand, so we would expect to find reductions in unstressed position, but not in stressed position. This is confirmed in Galician by the existence of phonemically contrastive open and closed mid vowels only in stress-related positions. It has been demonstrated that this situation transfers to Galician Spanish, although more contrastive studies need to be done. Castro (1998) confirmed Carballo Calero's (1979) insight that Galician only has contrastive open and closed middle vowels in stressed related positions. That is, we find lexical distinctions between open and closed mid vowels in tonic and pre-tonic syllables related to stress. We do not find a contrast between these vowels in the pre-tonic syllable immediately preceding the tonic unless that syllable is the first syllable of the word. In order to explain this contrast, Castro associated a secondary stress with word-initial position in Galician.

Carballo Calero states:

> El campo de entonación es más extenso en gallego que en castellano. Si en este idioma suele rebasar un poco una octava, en el nuestro alcanza más de dos. El tono medio es también más alto en gallego que en castellano. La riqueza melódica del gallego da al hablante castellano la sensación de que el hablante gallego canta. Esta sensación es particularmente intensa ante el dialecto suroccidental, en el que la curva melódica es más pronunciada que en el gallego del resto de Galicia. (1979, 147)

> [The field of intonation is more extensive in Galician that in Castilian. If in the latter it tends to go over an octave, in ours it reaches more than two. Average tone is also higher in Galician than Castilian. The melodic richness of Galician gives the Castilian speaker the impression that the Galician speaker sings when talking. This impression is particularly intense when confronted with the Southwestern dialect, where the melodic curve is more pronounced than in the rest of Galicia].[7]

According to Hirst and Di Cristo, "In a stress language the actual pitch accent associated with accented syllables may vary according to the intonation" (1998, 10). This is confirmed for Spanish, as we can see in Figure 4.3 below, where the word *hablar* "to speak," with stress on the final syllable, does not have a special pitch associated with it in the intonational contour, but the word *conmigo* "with me," with stress on the penultimate syllable, carries a high pitch on the first syllable *con*. The stressed syllable *mi* does not receive the highest pitch because it is at the end of the utterance and follows the expected falling contour identified for this position in Spanish.

At the word level, every word pronounced in isolation in Galician and Spanish has a specific word accent, even though some of these words never appear accented at the phrase level, i.e., *cómo* "how," *como* "I eat," *como* "as, like." The interrogative form *cómo* has a pitch accent to signal a question, the verb form *como* is stressed on the penultimate syllable, and the preposition does not show up stressed in the discourse (although it does have stress when pronounced in isolation and can receive phrasal stress if given emphasis). Only lexical words carry stress in both languages; the so-called grammatical words (prepositions, articles, etc.) do not carry stress.

Crystal (1969) defined "pitch onset" as a rising pitch in the first stressed syllable of the unit. The combination of rising onset and falling nucleus is a common feature of languages. It is also common to find a rising pitch on each stressed syllable, except the last. In Spanish and American English a falling rather than a rising pattern is common in stressed syllables.

Antonio Quilis (1988), in his study of Spanish intonation, identifies three tonal levels for Spanish: 1 (low), 2 (medium), and 3 (high), but in his analysis of the data, he only identifies 1 and 2 in most Spanish phrases. Tonal level 3 appears, according to Quilis, only when indicating emphasis, and in echo, relative, and imperative questions, as well as at the beginning of exclamations. Matluck (1965) establishes the following structure for simple declarative sentences in Spanish: /1211/. Galician seems to start higher, go up to level 3 or even 4 on stressed vowels, and never come down to a level lower than 2.

Another typological distinction relevant for our purposes is that of stress-timed vs. syllable-timed languages. Navarro Tomás (1939) views Spanish as a syllable-timed language. Fant (1984), on the other hand, considers Spanish as a stress-timed language similar to English and not as a syllable-timed language like Italian.

We also need to consider the difference between trailer-timed languages and leader-timed languages, as presented by Wenk and Wioland (1982). Trailer-timed languages create left-headed stress groups where the tonic syllable joins together with the following unstressed syllables to form the stress group. Leader-timed languages create right-headed stress groups where the tonic syllable joins with the preceding unstressed syllables to form the stress group. Standard Spanish appears to behave as a leader-timed language.[8] The difference between leader-timed (right-headed) and trailer-timed languages (left-headed) becomes relevant when we look at the differences between Brazilian Portuguese and European Portuguese. One of the differences between these two varieties is the fact that vowels in unstressed position tend to reduce more in European Portuguese than in Brazilian Portuguese. It is said also that Galician shares this particular characteristic with its neighbor to the South, and this is one of the differences between Spanish and Galician as well. If this is true, there is a correlation between a language having left-headed stress groups and reduction of vowels in unstressed position. We need to add that Galician does not go as far as European Portuguese in this respect.

Analysis

Porto Dapena (1977) reports on the observations made by Dámaso Alonso and García Yebra about a special word stress in Ancares Galician. According to these two scholars, besides the stress of intensity in Ancares Galician we have a tonal stress in the pre-tonic syllable, a situation they compare with French and Cuban Spanish. Porto Dapena did not find this in Ferrol Galician, stating that both these stresses fall on the tonic syllable when the word is pronounced in isolation. He adds, though, that the melodic curve varies according to the location of the stressed syllable within the word. What Porto Dapena calls tonal stress, we call pitch accent, and our hypothesis will be that it may be present or not at the word level, where it can coincide with the stressed syllable, but it will be present at the phrasal level. The high pitch associated with this position in Galician reappears in Galician Spanish through instances of open and closed mid vowels in those positions. This intensity or prominence is frequently correlated with duration. Prominent vowels sound longer and more intense. In our data, a bilingual speaker, when mimicking another speaker's utterances, clearly elongates the vowels. The original utterance was *yo sé de una casa que tiene habitaciones* "I know of a house that has rooms," with stress on the capitalized vowels of *yO, sE, cAsa, tiEne,* and *habitaciOnes* and a special pitch on the stressed vowels of *cAsa* and *habitaciOnes*. The second speaker, when imitating the intonation of the first, clearly elongates these vowels, actually saying *YO sE de una cÁsa que tiEne habitaciÕnes,* but the raising pitch contour is very noticeable as well. Nevertheless, as displayed in Figures 4.1 and 4.2, the difference in duration is not significant and does not seem to be a factor.

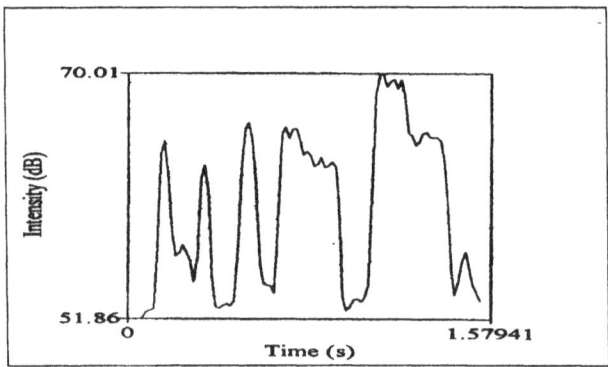

Figure 4.1. Intensity chart for *Se puso a hablar conmigo* "He engaged me in conversation" uttered by a non-Galician Spanish speaker

Stress and Intonation   43

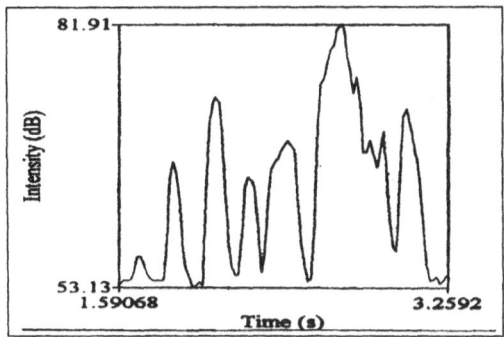

Figure 4.2. Intensity Chart for *Se puso a hablar conmigo* "He engaged me in conversation" uttered by a Galician Spanish speaker

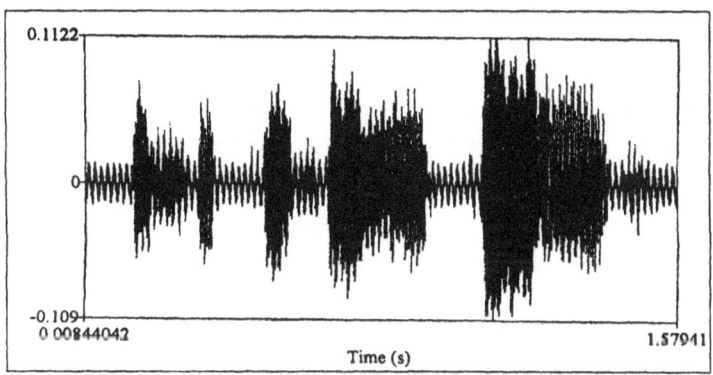

Figure 4.3. Spectrogram for *Se puso a hablar conmigo* "He engaged me in conversation" uttered by a Spanish speaker

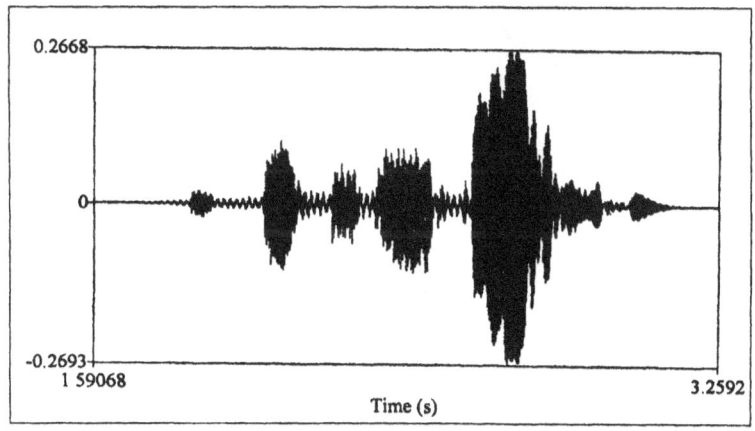

Figure 4.4. Spectrogram for *Se puso a hablar conmigo* "He engaged me in conversation" uttered by a Galician speaker

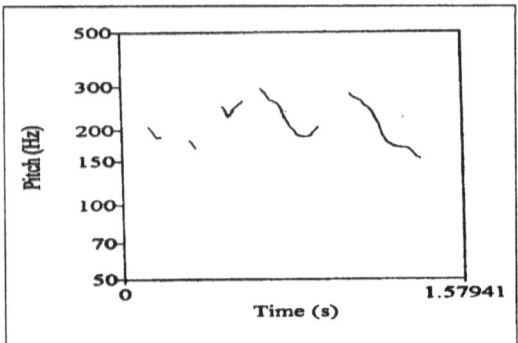

Figure 4.5. Pitch chart for *Se puso a hablar conmigo* "He engaged me in conversation" uttered by a Spanish speaker

In Figure 4.5 the intonation contour goes up to about 268 Hz in the first syllable *con* of *conmigo* "with me" and then drops to about 163 in the syllable *mi*. In Figure 4.6, the pitch contour goes up to about 288 Hz for *con*, and continues to rise up to about 380 Hz in *mi* and then drops slightly to about 342 in the last syllable *go*. We can see that even though there is a small fall at the end of the utterance in Galician Spanish, this falling movement stops rather quickly, and it does not go nearly as far down as it does in the Spanish example.

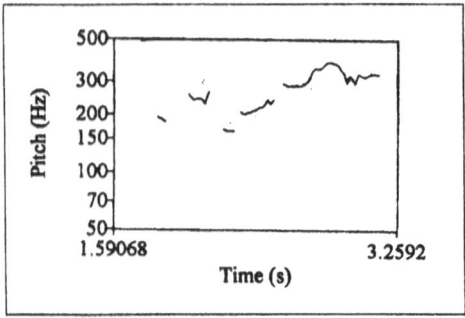

Figure 4.6. Pitch chart for *Se puso a hablar conmigo* "He engaged me in conversation" uttered by a Galician Spanish speaker

It has been generally agreed that a rising tone takes longer to produce than a falling tone. This could explain why the vowels are perceived as longer in Galician compared to standard Spanish, where accented vowels do not rise as much as in Galician but have a more pronounced drop. According to Hasegawa (1999), a falling tone needs to drop quite a bit in order to be identified as making a difference in the pitch contour. Since Galician does not seem to have a pronounced falling tone at the end of utterances, its final drop does not register for monolingual Spanish speakers.

Stress and Intonation 45

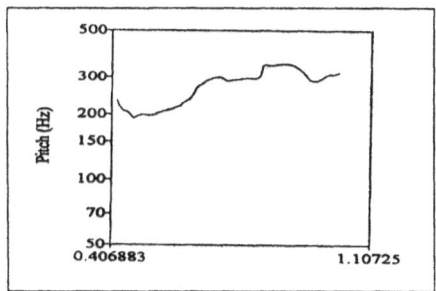

Figure 4.7. Pitch Chart of *como non ves...* "Since you are not coming..." uttered by a Galician speaker

[Note: The complete sentence pronounced was *Como non ves, imos sin ti* "Since you are not coming, we will go without you." Here only the pitch contour for the first part is represented.]

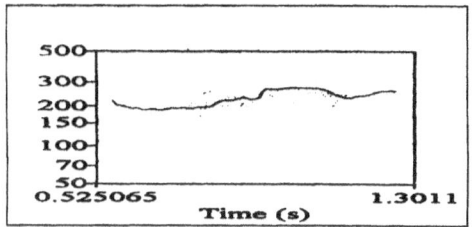

Figure 4.8. Pitch chart of *como no vienes...* "Since you are not coming..." uttered by a non Galician Spanish speaker

[Note: The complete sentence pronounced was *Como no vienes, iremos sin ti* "Since you are not coming, we will go without you." Here only the pitch contour for the first part is represented.]

Although Figures 4.7 and 4.8 look very similar, there are some noticeable differences. The pitch rises to 400 Hz in the Galician speaker, and it does not reach 300 Hz in the Spanish speaker. Since these examples are part of a longer phrase, the pitch remains higher in both speakers. This is what we would expect in an incomplete phrase as part of universal intonation typology. Notice that the Galician example surpasses 300 Hz, while the Spanish does not reach this level. It is interesting to note that impressionistic comments say that Spanish speakers "sing" when uttering unfinished phrases. The same comments are made about Galician in general, not only about unfinished phrases.

Questions formed with an interrogative word have been used as examples of a falling pitch in sentence final position in Spanish. We have a minimal pair in Galician and an almost minimal pair in Spanish with the form represented in Figures 4.7 and 4.8. In Figures 4.9 and 4.10 we can see the pitch contours for ¿*Cómo non ves?* in Galician and ¿*Cómo que no vienes?* in Spanish, "What do you mean you are not coming?" Although these two languages have a great deal in common, we were not able to find a perfect minimal pair for the Spanish version. Monolingual Castilian speakers reported they could not use ¿*Cómo?* "How?" with the meaning ¿*Por qué?* "Why?," which would be the way to say this phrase in Spanish: ¿*Por qué no vienes?* "Why are you not coming?" or "Why don't you come?" In Spanish, speakers reported that this phrase would be either stated using *Por qué* "Why" or it would have to be paraphrased as ¿*Y eso que no vienes?*, which is the closest semantic representation for the original Galician form. It is worth noting that monolingual Castilian speakers were not able to say ¿*Cómo no vienes?*, but Galician Spanish speakers had no problem with this form and were able to say it with the same meaning.

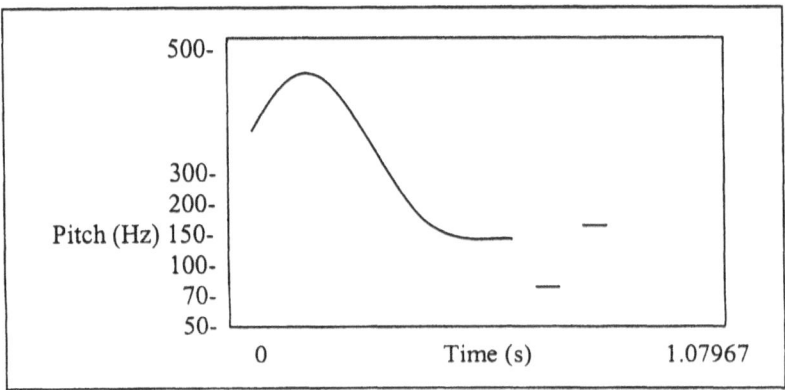

Figure 4.9. Pitch contour for ¿*Cómo non ves?* "What do you mean you are not coming?" uttered by a Galician speaker

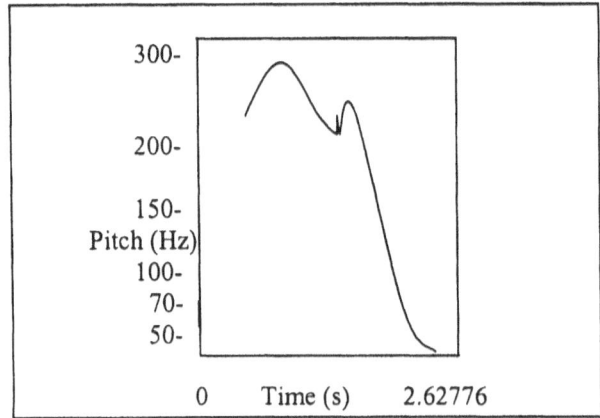

Figure 4.10. Pitch contour for ¿*Cómo que no vienes?* "What do you mean you are not coming?" uttered by a Spanish monolingual speaker

Observe the continuous and rapid fall for this question in Spanish. It reaches its highest peak at about 300 Hz and falls to about 80 Hz. Compare this figure with Figure 4.11, where the highest peak appears at more than 400 Hz and gradually drops to about 175 Hz in the stressed vowel *e* and remains at that level until the end of the utterance with no falling curve.

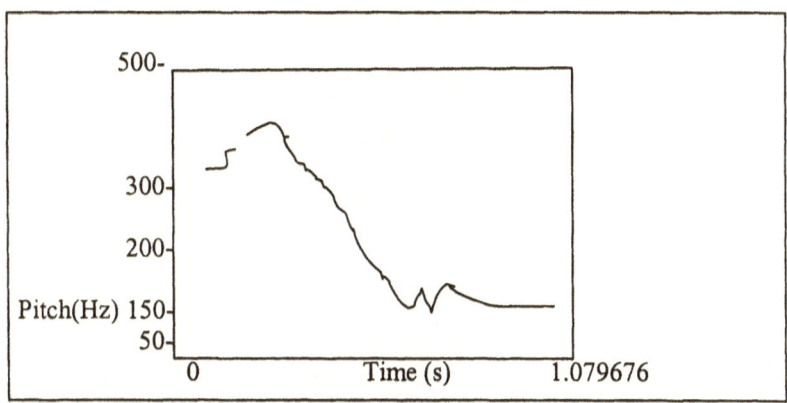

Figure 4.11. Pitch contour of *¿Cómo que no vienes?* "What do you mean you are not coming?" uttered by a bilingual Galician Spanish speaker

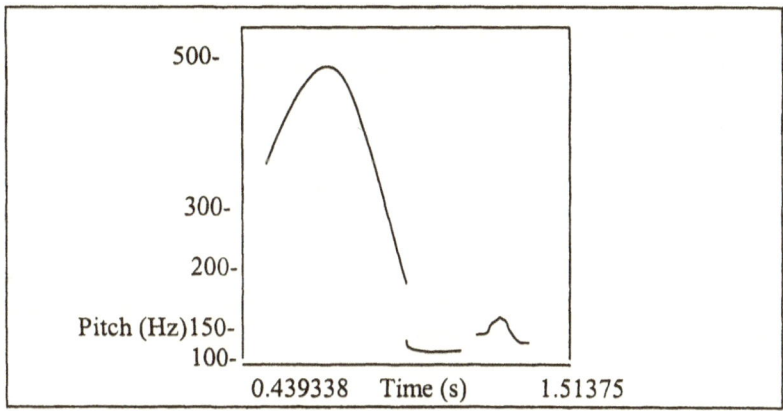

Figure 4.12. Pitch contour of *¿Cómo no vienes?* "What do you mean you are not coming?" uttered in Spanish by a bilingual Galician Spanish speaker

Notice that the contour on Figure 4.12 resembles the one in Figure 4.9. Even though the speaker is using a different language (Galician in 4.9, Spanish in 4.12), the intonation contour remains the same. If we compare these two figures with Figure 4.10, we can see that this question has a fall in all varieties considered, but the fall is continuous and steep in Spanish, while it is not so pronounced in Galician and Galician Spanish, where if it goes down in one part of the utterance, it comes back up on the last stressed vowel.

Summing up, we can say that in questions both Galician and Galician Spanish start higher than Spanish, and although there is a fall in questions, this fall is not as pronounced as in Spanish.

Other areas of the Spanish-speaking world have been associated with a rising pitch at the end of utterances, among them the Argentinian varieties of Tucumán and Córdoba (Alcoba and Murillo, 1998). Tucumán speech has been identified as having only two terminal contours; rising and level. It has been said that speakers of Buenos Aires perceive statements uttered by speakers of Tucumán as questions, due to the very high pitch encompassing even unstressed syllables. Within Spain itself, the speech of Extremadura has been described as having a high pitch at the end (Alcoba and Murillo, 1998).[9]

Conclusions and Further Research

In Galician, regardless of syntactic, semantic, or affective meaning, stress and pitch work together to give special prominence to the last accented syllable in the phrase, while in Spanish, pitch is mostly used to mark syntactic, semantic, or affective meaning. Also, although there is a rise-fall pitch contour in all accented vowels in Galician, the pitch contour signaling the end of an utterance in Galician is clearly marked by a high on the accented vowel, and a very short-lived fall on the following syllable (if there is one). The rising tone in Galician is higher than in Spanish, and the falling tone does not go as far down. It levels off midway, thereby giving the impression to speakers of other languages that the speaker has not finished his/her turn. The boundary is signaled in Galician by a final sentence pitch accent.

In this chapter, we have reported on preliminary data that points to a special pitch accent in utterance final position in Galician Spanish. More research needs to be done to confirm these findings. These studies will shed some light on the directionality of stress groups in Galician and Galician Spanish and help us determine if Galician Spanish aligns itself with European Portuguese or Spanish.

We have also shown evidence that intonation is acquired rather early and once acquired stays with the speaker regardless of L1. The clearly distinct Galician intonation observed in speakers of Spanish from Galicia is a good example of this.

Notes

1. See section on diminutive formation for more information on these forms.

2. An earlier version of this section was published in *Selected Proceedings of the First Workshop in Spanish Sociolinguistics*, Lotfi Sayahi, ed., Cascadilla Proceedings Project, 2003, with the title "Pitch Accent in Galician Spanish."

3. This study only looks at one side of intonation in these languages in contact. It will be left for another study to look at the Castilian intonation present in some speakers of Galician. This particular intonation can be explained by making reference to a stage in the learning process: language learners who do not have complete control of the language yet, or by native speaker's perception (by choice or by imposition of the local and

national cultural elite) of what is considered to be the prestigious variety. For some speakers of Galician (native and learners alike), it is now fashionable and politically correct to speak Galician, but it sounds more educated when all characteristics internal to Galician are eliminated and the accent approximates Castilian as much as possible. It is interesting to see that in the regional media, newscasters speak Galician with a Castilian accent, but in programs imported from England, when needing to dub the voices of Cockney speakers, an attempt is made to represent it with characteristics of Galician associated with low registers of prestige. As it was previously mentioned, this will be the subject of another study.

4. I extend my sincere gratitude to the Instituto for allowing me to copy a significant number of their materials.

5. PRAAT, a speech analysis tool for doing phonetics on the computer, was used. This shareware program was developed by Paul Boersma of the University of Amsterdam and can be downloaded at www.praat.org.

6. It is interesting to note that major changes in vowel quality in Spanish stressed or unstressed vowels are only found in situations where Spanish is in contact with other languages.

7. Unless otherwise noted, all translations are my own.

8. Alcoba and Murillo consider Spanish "to behave like a trailer-timed language. The tonic syllables group together with the preceding unstressed syllables to constitute a unit which behaves differently from the syllable or the foot" (1998, 166). They probably mean to say that Spanish is a leader-timed language, according to their definition.

9. It would be interesting to study whether there is any relationship between low prestige varieties and final raising pitch. So far, all the varieties mentioned here seem to have low prestige in their own linguistic communities.

V.
The Obligatory Contour Principle and the Pronoun System of Spanish: Syntax, Morphology, and Phonology at the Crossroads

As we have been saying, the interleaving of levels makes it very difficult to keep morphology and phonology separate. In the pronoun system in Spanish, this situation becomes even more complicated by the role played by the syntax in the placement of these forms within the sentence.

In Spanish we find one form for the indirect object pronoun *le* "to him, to her, to you (formal)" as in *Le di el libro* "I gave him/her, or you (formal) the book." Spanish requires that when two object pronouns are used together, the indirect object pronoun must precede the direct object pronoun, and they can be placed before a conjugated verb as two different words or attached as a single word after an infinitive or a present participle. Following these rules, we would expect to find a form like **le lo di or ***dálelo,* but instead we find *se lo di* "I gave it to him/her/ or you (formal)" and *dáselo* "give it to him/her or you (formal)."

In traditional Spanish grammar textbooks for foreign language learners, these occurrences are explained as a restriction on the appearance of two consecutive object pronouns beginning with *l* appearing together. This is a good example of identity avoidance in the output of pre-posed and post-posed placement of direct and indirect object pronouns as observed in examples such as 1) *se lo da* "Third person or second person formal gives it (masc.) to third person or second person formal (sing. or pl.)," and 2) *dáselo* "Command second person informal 'give it' (masc.) to third person or second person formal singular or plural."

In examples 1) and 2), *se* is the output manifestation of the indirect object pronoun *le* prevented from appearing in the surface by a constraint on the presence of two "ls" in continuous syllables. This example of what can be called dissimilation in traditional terminology causes the indirect object pronoun to manifest itself as *se* instead of *le*. This process cannot be explained as an example of simplification, since the resulting form now conflicts with the reflexive *se* as well as with other *se* uses in Spanish, such as in impersonal expressions: *se cortan las verduras* "the vegetables are cut," the dative of interest: *se me cayó* "it fell down and it happened to me," etc. Processes like the *le* to *se* change can be explained with the obligatory contour principle postulated by Leben (1973). It is of special interest to see that this restriction involves segments not only in different syllables and morphemes, but different words as well, and it does not seem to be affected by the intervening vowels. This restriction appears to be only applicable to these two pronouns in sequence, since we have plenty of examples of words with these exact forms: *paralelo* "parallel," *paralelismo* parallelism," etc., where the restriction seems to have no effect.

Historically, these forms evolved through a series of steps. Menéndez Pidal (1973) explains the evolution of the forms *se lo* from the juxtaposition of the Latin masculine and feminine dative *illi* and the Latin masculine accusative *illum*. From *illi illum* he posits *(i)lliello* as an intermediate derivation that evolved to *gelo* pronounced [zelo]. He also explains that the plural regular form *leslo* patterns itself after *gelo,* therefore losing the difference between singular and plural in these forms. This loss of the plural marker has created a certain instability in the current Spanish system, and utterances such as **díselos* "tell it to them" or **se los dije* "I told it to them" are becoming quite common. In these forms, the plural marker, absent in *se*, is re-positioned in *los*. In the standard forms *díselo* and *se lo dije*, the direct object pronoun *lo* maintains its singular form. Expressions such as *dile a ellos que...* "tell them that..." can also be seen as attempts to deal with the absence/presence of the plural marker, but in this case, we have an attempt at avoiding re-duplication or redundancy, as standard Spanish calls for the plural marker to be present in both the indirect object clitic pronoun and the object of a preposition personal pronoun form: *diles a ellos que...*[1] According to Menéndez Pidal 1973), the form *selo* comes from morphological analogy with the reflexive *se*.[2] This gives us a good description of the process of evolution but no insight into why this should be the case.

We could also hypothesize that the form *selo* did not evolve from the singular form, but from the plural form itself with the re-syllabification of the final *s* of *illis* to the next syllable, and the elimination of *illi*. This hypothetical evolution is represented in Table 5.1.

The Obligatory Contour Principle and the Pronoun System of Spanish   53

Table 5.1. Hypothetical evolution of *illis illum* to *se lo*

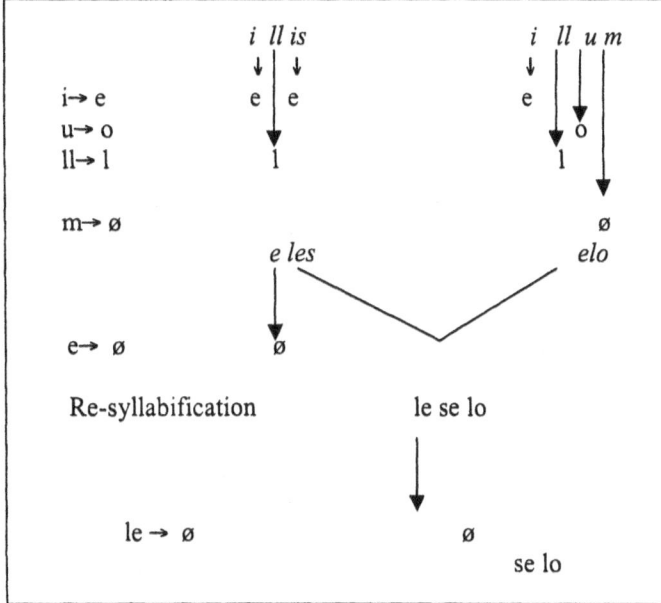

This derivation would explain why the plural is no longer expressed in these forms. It is actually already there re-syllabified. We could say that it was this re-syllabified plural form, the one that was taken over by the singular because of its similarity with the already existing reflexive *se*.

We need to emphasize that this is just a hypothetical derivation, and it will have to remain so until we establish more grounds to justify it, but it would explain why the plural information seems to have been lost.

We would also like to venture the hypothesis of the Identity Avoidance Principle as playing a role in this process. This principle has been used to explain the non-occurrence of similar segments together. Following Yip's (1998) suggestion, we have been using *REPEAT as a constraint that reflects exactly this principle. As we have seen, *REPEAT works not only at the segmental level, avoiding repetition of contiguous segments, but also at the morphological level, avoiding repetition of morphemes. Yip (1998) states that the Obligatory Contour Principle prevents dative *ko* and an acusative *ko* from surfacing together in Japanese.

Spanish is well known for not having geminate consonants. All of the geminates from Latin were reduced and sometimes lost in Spanish. The juxtaposition of *illi illum* was no exception, as the double *l*s were reduced to just one: *ilielo*. The process undergone by *lie* to become *se* eventually can be looked at as one way of not allowing two consecutive onsets to begin with the same consonant.

On occasion we encounter instances of similar segments together without the intervention of the OCP. We have seen such instances in the diminutive formation of words such as *rio-riito* "river-small river," *tia-tiita* "aunt-small (dear) aunt." The OCP is prevented from applying here because doing so would make these forms impossible to relate to their original form. A better way to explain this would to say that *Repeat is outranked by Recovery.

It is interesting that a phenomenon which started historically as a possible example of the OCP can be explained synchronically today as an example of the same principle.

We could postulate a constraint called *R-Onset according to which identical contiguous onsets would not be allowed. This constraint would prevent **dalelo* from surfacing. allowing *dáselo* "give it to him" to surface instead. It could be expected that this constraint would prevent the appearance of onset *l* in two consecutive syllables, but this is not the case. This constraint would not allow standard forms such as *paralelo* "parallel" or *lelo* "dumb" to surface, clearly indicating that this constraint does not restrict segments in word-internal or initial position. It also does not restrict the appearance of two *l*s across word boundaries. We have forms like *le levanta* "he/she/you (formal) raise him/her/you (formal)." *Se levanta* "he/she/you (formal) cause himself/herself/yourself (formal) to get up" has a different meaning and is not an example of the action of this principle. In order for this principle to take effect, the forms affected have to be precisely the two object pronouns in question. Consider that "*le*" and "*lo*" are not forms to be added to a word to change its meaning, that is, they are not affixes. Instead they are parts of speech, although not independent.

The prohibition for *le lo* to appear together only applies to the clitic form of the aforementioned pronouns. These clitics work here as phonological domains. In some registers of fast speech we encounter expressions such as *golelo* for *olerlo* "to smell it." These forms are never changed to *selo* because the *le* is not an instance of the indirect object pronoun. In this case, *le* is part of the root of the verb, and we have only one instance of the direct object pronoun *lo*.

Another possible example of the action of the OCP in Spanish can be observed in the diminutive forms of words such as *tomate-tomatico* "tomato-small tomato" instead of *tomatito, gato-gatico* "cat-small cat" instead of *gatito*. These forms are typical of Aragon in Spain, Costa Rica, and Venezuela.

We have to admit that such recalcitrant examples as the prohibition of **lelo(a)* to appear together as clitic object pronouns are unique peculiarities of the language that will probably never find a complete explanation within any linguistic theory, but regardless of the approach we use, we have to keep trying to see if we can explain what appear to be anomalous phenomena as part of Universal Grammar.

Notes

1. We need to note that the source of the redundancy here lies in the required duplication or copying of two object pronouns with the same meaning in Spanish. The standard *Diles a ellos que...* literally means "Tell them to them that..." It is interesting that for speakers who say **dile a ellos*, the duplication of the pronoun takes precedence

over the duplication of the plural marker; the plural marker can be eliminated to avoid redundancy, but the same is not true for the duplication of the pronoun.

2. See also Lloyd (1987) and Lathrop (1984, 1996), among others.

VI.
The Acquisition of Alternating Diphthongs in Native and Non-Native Systems

The so-called alternating diphthongs in Spanish have been the object of numerous studies within the field of Spanish linguistics. We need only consider a few of those, such as Harris (1969, 1983, 1985, 1995) and Carreira (1991), to observe how different the approaches used to explain these diphthongs can be.

The term "alternating diphthongs" is used to identify forms that alternate the presence of a diphthong with the presence of a simple vowel depending on the placement of stress. This phenomenon is typical of a good number of verbs, nouns, adjectives, etc.

Verbs (present indicative)

tener "to have"	*volver* "to return"	*sentir* "to feel"	*dormir* "to sleep"
tengo[1] "I have"	*vuelvo* "I return"	*siento* "I feel"	*duermo* "I sleep"
tienes "you have"	*vuelve* "you return"	*sientes* "you feel"	*duermes* "you sleep"
tenemos "we…"	*volvemos* "we…"	*sentimos* "we…"	*dormimos* "we…"
tenéis "you…"	*volvéis* "you…"	*sentís* "you…"	*dormís* "you…"
tienen "they…"	*vuelven* "they…"	*sienten* "they…"	*duermen* "they…"

Nouns

piedra "stone"	*mueble* "piece of furniture"	*diente* "tooth"	*fuente* "fountain"
pedrada "stone-blow"	*mobiliario* "furnishings"	*dentista* "dentist"	*fontanero* "plumber"

Exceptions to these alternations

Pedro[2] "Peter"	*mueblería* "furniture store"	*dientito* "small tooth"	*fuentecita* "small fountain"

Adjectives

fiel "faithful"	bueno "good"	miel "honey"	huelga "strike"
Fidelidad[3] "faithfulness"	bondad "goodness"	meloso "honey-like"	holgazán "lazy"

Adverbs

fielmente "faithfully"	buenamente "kindly"	bien "well"	luego "then, soon"

This alternation is usually associated with the presence or absence of stress on the position associated with the diphthong. When the vowel is stressed, we find the diphthong: *fiesta* "party"; when the vowel is unstressed, we find just one vowel: *festejo* "celebration." This is not an absolute process, as we have a number of exceptions: *fiestero* "party lover," *fiestecita* "small party." As we will see when discussing diminutive formation, the appearance of the diphthong in forms where the diphthong is not in stressed position is explained through the addition of the affix at the lexeme level, not at the word level. Everything seems to indicate that this is also the case for the suffix *–ero (a)*, according to forms such as *fiestero*.

The Native System

In order to see how the previously described alternating forms are learned in the L1 context, we used the corpus created by López Ornat (1994). Her team videotaped and transcribed the language used by a Spanish girl from 1:07 to 4:00 years of age. From this data we scanned all the forms with and without alternating diphthongs. We extracted target and non-target examples of alternating forms as well as forms with *–o–* and *–e–* in a position similar to that of alternating diphthongs.

Beginning at the age of 1:07, we find **tene* for *tiene* "he/she/it has," **pé* for *pie* "foot," and **pés* for *pies* "feet." At 1:09 we find **mé* for *bien* "well, good" and the target forms *siento, sienta* for *me siento* "I sit down," *se sienta* "he/she/it sits down," *llueve* "it rains," *pie* "foot." From 1:10-3:00 we find a few instances of non-target *–o–* and *–e–* with an increasing number of target *–ue–* and *–ie–*. There are very few examples of non-target forms at 3:00, and by 3:09 most instances are target-like. One interesting point to mention is the small number of errors in non-alternating forms. We only encountered one instance of **guompe* for *rompe* "he/she/it breaks," which is a non-alternating verb, and one instance of **pieltas* for *puertas* "doors," where the wrong alternating diphthong is used. We also found one instance of **perta* for *puerta* "door," where the wrong root vowel appears. All other examples found in the corpus studied here have an outstanding target-like presence of variation only in alternating forms. The correspondence of *o–ue*, and *e–ie* is also almost without exception. We did not find examples of non-alternating verbs showing alternations. This is a very striking difference from the non-native learners, where we find many examples of mixing between the two groups, with a larger number of mixing candidates at the beginning stages and an increasingly smaller number of candidates at the advanced stages.

A few examples in the data deserve some observations: The form *guompe* is the only example we found where a non-alternating verb showed the presence of a diphthong in stressed position. The target form is *rompe* with an –*o*– in stressed position, as we would expect of non-alternating verbs. What is interesting about the example from our data is the fact that the diphthong produced in this case is not –*ue*–, but rather –*uo*–. Carreira (1991) considers that *uo* and not *ue* was the original diphthong found in these forms. The *ue* in contemporary forms is produced, according to Carreira, because of *uo*'s violation of the Obligatory Contour Principle in Spanish, which prohibits the sequence of vowels with the same value for feature [dorsal].[4] Carreira uses this principle to explain the monophthongization of *ie–e* and *ue–o*.

We also have a very good example of paradigmatic regularization in the form *tieno* for the standard *tengo*. This last form is a good example of what Bybee (1994) has called "fossilized sound change from bygone eras." This form is part of a group of verbs with irregular first person singular forms. The child in the corpus we are studying converts the first person singular of *tener* "to have" into a more regular form following the paradigm of verbs like *querer–quiero* "to want–I want." This type of formation is a clear indication that although phenomena like the alternating diphthongs in Spanish need to be learned and are not part of productive processes, they are still considered as more regular than more distant learned forms like *tengo*. This seems to indicate that between learned paradigms there is a clear distinction between those far removed from new manipulation and those that are closer to the regularizing control of the speaker. Although we do not see new alternating diphthong verbs being formed, we can observe that native speakers appear to be aware of their existence and prefer to create regular paradigms using their forms, as opposed to more fossilized ones. We can conclude that some fossilized sound changes are more fossilized than others.

From López Ornat (1994) we counted all forms of target and non-target alternating diphthongs until the age of 3:07. After this age all forms were target, and we decided to stop counting them. In Table 6.1 we can see how the production of target forms increases with age. By age 1:07, only 29% of the forms produced are target forms for the *e–ie* alternation. By age 2, the number of target forms increases to 42.4%, and by age 3 it reaches 83.3%. Remember that after age 3:07 all forms encountered were target forms.

The Acquisition of Alternative Diphthongs in Native and Non-Native Systems

Table 6.1. Native Acquisition of Alternating Diphthongs *e–ie*

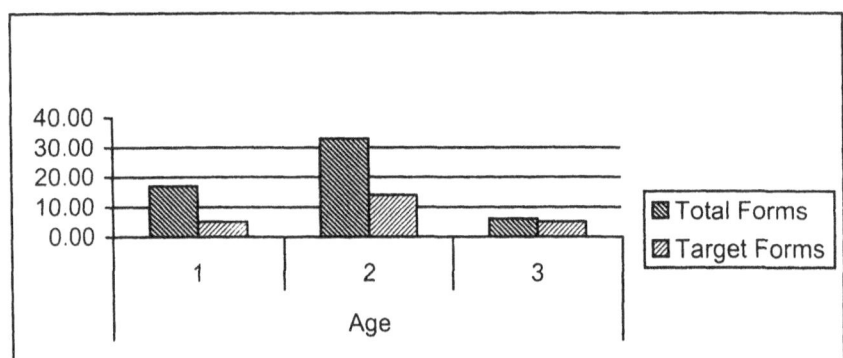

If we compare Table 6.2 to Table 6.1, we find something surprising. We would tend to think that the rate of acquisition for the two alternating diphthongs would be the same, but from the results of this study, we can see that the number of utterances produced with the alternating form *o–ue* is rather small at age 1:07 when compared with the number of utterances produced at age 1:00 for *e–ie*. The number of utterances is about the same at age 2 and then levels off at age 3:00. Not only are the amounts different, but the percentage of target and non-target forms is also very different. At age 1:07, the percentages of target forms are about the same for the two alternations: 29% for *e–ie* and 28.5% for *o–ue*, but the number of utterances is very different. At age 1, there were 59% fewer instances of words with the alternating diphthong *o–ue* than with the alternating diphthong *e–ie*. At age 2, the number of productions level off for both alternations, and by age 3, the alternation *o–ue* has 68.5% more instances than *e–ie*. This appears to indicate that these two forms are not acquired at the same time, at least not at the same rate.

We find another striking difference in the relationship between target and non-target forms. In *e–ie* we observed a progressive increase in the number of target forms until the age of 3:07, where they were all target forms. In the process of acquisition of the alternation *o–ue* we see a small number of target forms, 28.5%, at age 1, which is to be expected, but instead of steadily increasing at age 2, they actually decrease to 26.6%. By age 3:07 they reach 31.5%, and after that all utterances become target at 100%.

Table 6.2. Native Acquisition of Alternating Diphthongs *o–ue*

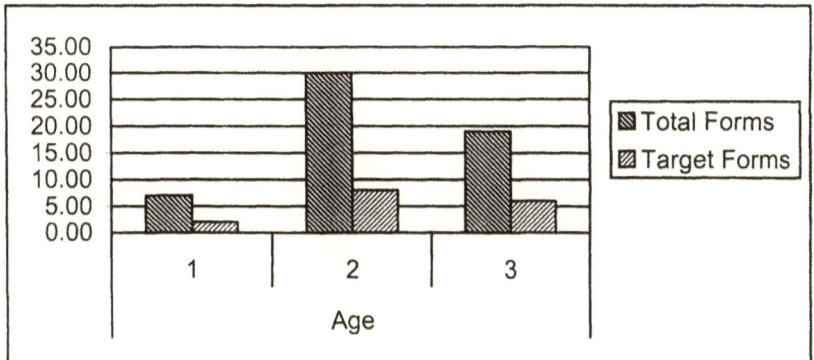

From the outset of the first few *o–ue* alternating forms to the achievement of 100% accuracy we have a period of 22 months where the percentage of targets does not get higher than 31%, and then all of the sudden total accuracy is reached. This seems to reflect a process similar to that described by López Ornat (1994, 115):

1. Pre-grammatical categorization—characterized by few errors and imitation. This would happen during year 1 for *e–ie* and *o–ue*.
2. Grammaticalization—a prototype is selected, year 2 for *e–ie*, but somehow the process is longer for *o–ue*. Actually, for the latter, year 2 is a continuation of pre-grammatical categorization.
3. Rigid Rule—overgeneralization errors, beginning of year 3 for *e–ie*. It is delayed for *o–ue*.
4. Flexible rule—absence of errors, by age 3:07 for both alternations.

Table 6.3 shows how the percentage of target forms increases steadily for *e–ie* but remains about the same for *o–ue*. The two begin in the same way at age 1, but after that it seems like *e–ie* takes center stage and *o–ue* remains in the background.

Table 6.3. Native Percentage of Target Forms 1-3 Years

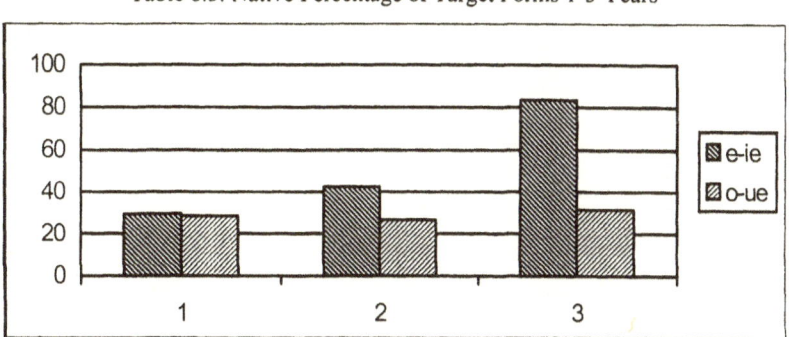

62   The Acquisition of Alternative Diphthongs in Native and Non-Native Systems

Table 6.4 shows the percentage of target forms for *e–ie* and *o–ue* from 1:07-3:07, the entire period where our study is concentrated. We can see that *e–ie* reaches 42.8% of target forms, while *o–ue* reaches only 29%. Nevertheless, both alternating forms become 100% target at about the same time.

Table 6.4. Comparison of Percentage of Target Forms for *ie* and *ue*

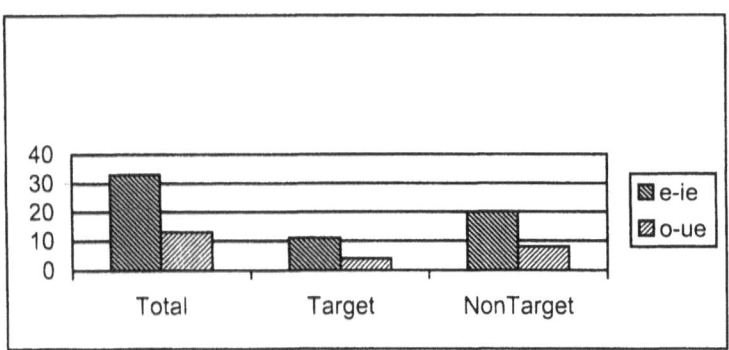

The previous odd results made us decide to look more closely at the period between 1:07-2:01, where a higher number of instances for *e–ie* was initially detected.

Table 6.5. Production of Forms with Alternating Diphthongs, 1:07-2:01

When looking at the whole period object of our study, we find the same number of utterances for both alternating forms. When we look more closely at the period between 1:07 and 2:01, a different picture emerges. During this period, the number of utterances for *e–ie* is almost three times larger than the one for *o–ue*: 33 instances of *e–ie*, 13 of *o–ue*, but when we look in Table 6.6 at the percentages of target and non-target forms for both alternations, they are surprisingly similar. We have a larger number of examples and a larger number of non-target forms for *e–ie* than for *o–ue* at this stage, but the relationship between target and non-target forms remains about the same. Although there are slightly more target forms of *e–ie*, the percentage of non-target forms is exactly the same for both alternations.

Table 6.6. Native System from 1:07-2:01, % of Target/Non-Target Forms

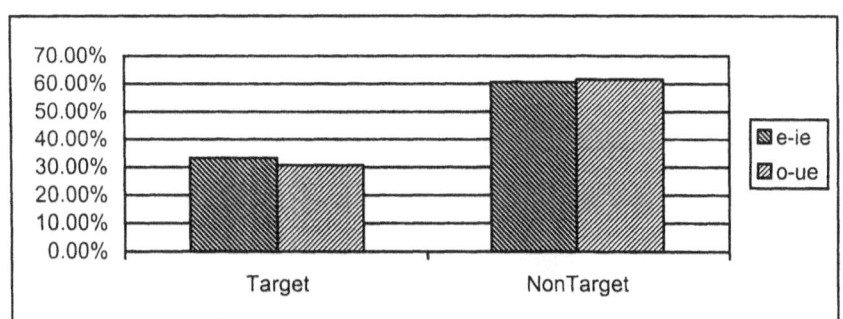

The Non-Native System

In order to see how non-native Spanish learners acquired and controlled alternating diphthongs, a study was conducted with first-semester college students studying Spanish at a major U.S. university. After four weeks of presentation and practice with the alternating verbs encountered in a typical first year Spanish textbook, students were given a list of known and unknown verbs and were asked to give the third person form for each of them.[5]

In Table 6.7 the first thing to see is that the order of acquisition seems to be different in L1 learners and L2 learners. For one thing, L2 learners seem to have a better control of *o–ue* than they do *e–ie*. This is the reverse of what we just saw in the previous section.

Table 6.7. L2 Acquisition of Alternating Diphthongs (First Semester)

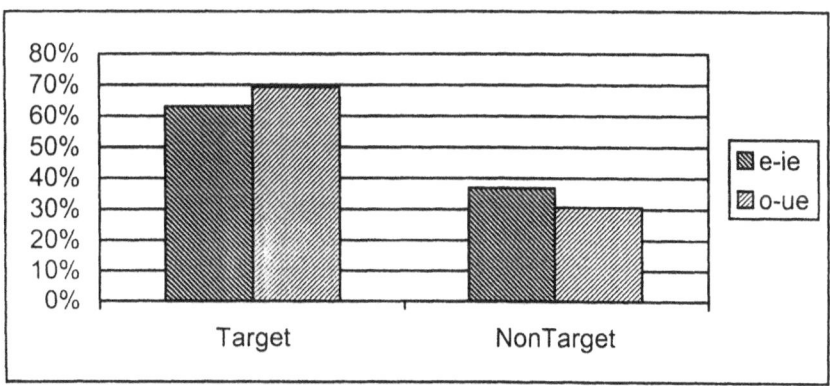

But if we compare Table 6.8 to Table 6.6, we see that the percentage of target and non-target forms in L2 learners resembles the percentages encountered in the L1 learner from 1:07 to 2:01, the only difference being that results are reversed for the two alternating forms. *o–ue* has a higher number of forms and a higher number of target forms than *e–ie*. This is just the opposite situation described for L1.

Table 6.8. Comparison of Totals vs. Target Forms in L2

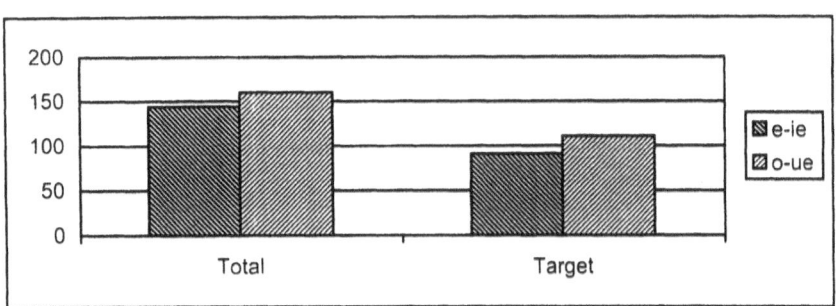

It could be argued that the difference in numbers comes from a higher number of examples in the L2 study. This is not the case, however, as care was taken to keep the numbers of forms the same. It just happens that the L2 learners had more target forms in *o–ue* than in *e–ie*. The difference in the number of forms comes from cases where no form was chosen for *e–ie*. When adding the total number of forms present, the results come higher on the side of *o–ue*, and this is not due to an excess of forms in this last category.

The Acquisition of Other Diphthongs in L2

With the purpose of gathering data on L2 acquisition of other diphthongs besides alternating diphthongs, a study was conducted at a major U. S. university. As part of this study, one group of students enrolled in a first-semester Spanish class and another group enrolled in a third-year Spanish class were asked to write a short paragraph dictated to them in Spanish. After writing down what they heard, they were asked to separate the words into syllables and write any accent mark they considered necessary. We will henceforth refer to this as the "*Eusebio* study." The purpose of the study was to analyze the level of acquisition of syllable structure, stress assignment, and discrimination of specific sounds.

In Tables 6.9 and 6.11 we can see the different utterances produced by students in the first-semester class. The first noteworthy finding from the results of this group is the consistent absence of a diphthong on the first syllable of the word *Eusebio*. This form was not pronounced in isolation, occurring as part of the flow of speech right after the word *amigo* "friend." If pronounced within the flow of speech right after an open vowel in the previous syllable, the untrained listener may not perceive the glide –u– in this context. 33.3% of the students chose to represent what they heard with an –a–, while 33.3% were not able to write anything.

Table 6.9. Sample Results for [ew] in the First-Semester Group

only *a*	(7) 33.3%
a with a consonant	(2) 9.5%
a as a different word	(2) 9.5%
only *au*	(2) 9.5%
only *y*	(1) 4.7%
only *u*	(1) 4.7%
y as a different word	(1) 4.7%
No form produced	(7) 33.3%

Table 6.10. Sample Results for [ew] in the Third-Year Group

only *eu*	(20) 95.0%
only *e.o*	(1) 4.7%
only *e.ii*	(1) 4.7%
only *au*	(1) 4.7%

The perception and syllabification of this falling diphthong *eu* by third-year students is quite accurate: 95% of the students were able to identify and reproduce this form correctly in writing.

L2 Acquisition of Falling and Rising Diphthongs

Table 6.11. Results for [ew] in the First-Semester Group

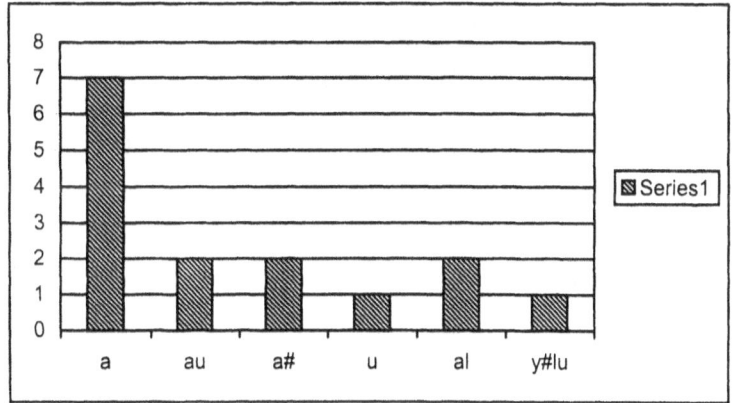

In the first-semester group we found no target instances of the falling diphthong *eu*. Most of the students identified this form with the vowel *a*, unable to perceive and represent a diphthong in this position. Comparing the perception of this diphthong with the rising diphthong *io*, we can see that it was much more difficult for students to perceive the falling diphthong than the rising one. This says something about the saliency of the beginning and endings of words for language learners. It seems that these students are able to discriminate glides at the end of words slightly better than glides at the beginning. Interestingly enough, they were able to perceive two vocalic elements in this position, while they were only able to identify a single vowel in beginning position. The problems encountered had to do with syllabification: they identified the two vocalic elements at the end with independent vowels, and not with an independent vowel and a vocoid.

Table 6.12. Results for [ew] in the Third-Year Group

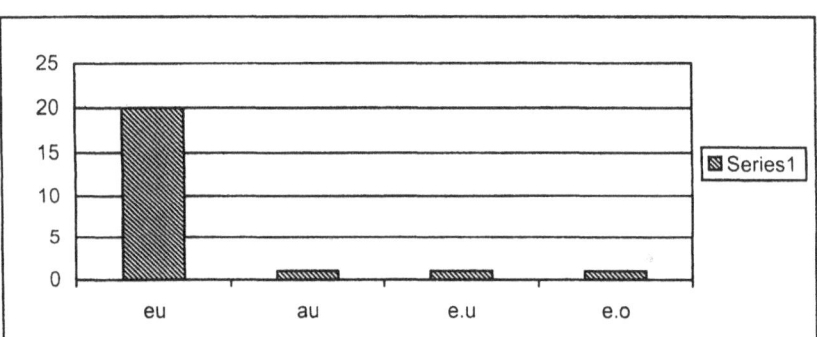

Third-year students were able to identify the diphthong at the beginning of the word with high levels of accuracy, and a high majority of these students were able to syllabify them correctly.

Students in first semester were very inconsistent in representing the diphthong *io*. Only a handful was able to recognize it as a diphthong. The majority of the group was either not able to syllabify it or not able to represent it altogether. Regardless of this, they represented this diphthong better than the falling diphthong at the beginning of the word.

Table 6.13. [jo] First Semester

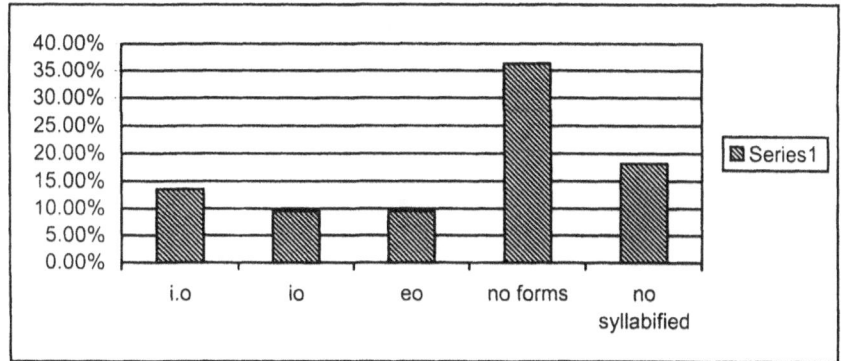

When it came to identifying the final rising diphthong, even though a large number of students were able to identify this form as a diphthong, we still have a high percentage of students who are not able to syllabify this form correctly. They still perceive two independent vowels in this position or have problems with syllabifying this form.

Table 6.14. [jo] Third Year

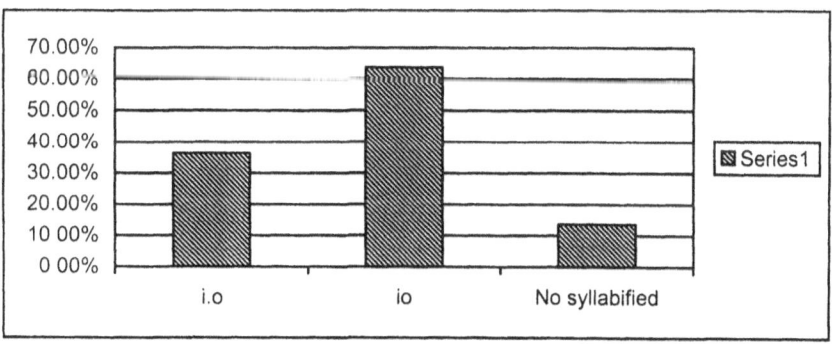

The difference in level of acquisition of these forms tells us that rising diphthongs seem to be more difficult to identify as such. Students tend to perceive two vowels in this position. Acquisition of Spanish syllable structure is still inconsistent in these forms. This is not surprising, since these forms are among the hardest to identify for L2 learners. This serves as a very good point of comparison with the L1 learning system, where these forms are developed quite early.

Notes

1. This form is irregular in the first person. See information below.
2. Compare Italian *Pietro*.
3. Notice that here the alternation is between –*i*– and –*ie*– instead of –*e*– and –*ie*–.
4. Words like *cuota* "share, fee, installment" and *alicuota* "aliquot" come to mind, but we have to agree that they are far from typical Spanish words.
5. See Doyle, Polly (2001), "La representación de los diptongos crecientes en los verbos españoles," University of Colorado, Boulder, ms.

VII.
Inflection vs. Derivation

Inflection and derivation are morphological processes by which a morpheme is added to an existing form. In the traditional literature, inflection has been studied as the addition of a morpheme without changing word categories, stress placement, etc. In Spanish, person endings in verbs have been studied as examples of inflection. Plural formation and gender assignment have also been considered examples of inflection. These assumptions have been based on the fact that these are mostly straightforward additions without changing the original form in any considerable way.

While inflection is not supposed to create new words, derivation has been considered as a morphological process which takes over the creation of new words. According to this, *casa* "house" is a word inflected with grammatical gender, while *casero* "landlord" is a denominal derivation of *casa* with the addition of a derivative affix *–er*, which now carries the stress of the new word. We can add the inflectional suffix for plural and form both *casas* "houses" and *caseros* "landlords," with the information related to gender remaining intact for both words. The addition of the plural morpheme does not change either the word category of these forms, as both are still nouns, nor the placement of stress. This is one of the reasons why number specification has been considered as an example of an inflectional process.

This sounds simple, but when we dig a little deeper, we realize that this not the case. Diminutive formation is such an example: it is straightforward enough, and it does not change the category of the word, but on the other hand, it does change stress placement, and it adds a special meaning to the word. It seems that this process has elements of both derivation and inflection.

It has been generally agreed that if there is a change in word category, we have an example of a derivational process, and a division was established between those derivational processes that affected stress placement and those that did not. A typical example of this has been the formation of adjective forms with the suffix *–ic*, which systematically retain the stress on the base of the original word. This is another way of saying that for some reason this affix does not affect the original stress of the word to which it is added. This affix behaves like a quasi-terminal element. Observe that it is not an absolute terminal element, because it can be followed by gender and number markings, which will appear without exception at the end of the word in Spanish.

All we need to say about words formed with *-ic* is that the suffix is added to a root and it does not affect stress placement. If we recall that we consider that the diminutive affix is added to the lexeme, we can see a difference in these two examples of word formation. We still need to pay attention to why forms such as *práctico(a)* "practical," *socrático(a)* "socratic," *pragmático(a)* "pragmatical," etc., failed to attract stress to them. We can attempt a number of different approaches to try to explain these facts. We can resort to historical information and find out that these are Latinate forms, which would explain their special behavior, but what we really need to do is to try to explain their usage from a synchronic point of view and to make them accessible to the learning system. Suffixation with *-ic* is absolutely regular, and learners of L1 as well as L2 find enough information in the learning system to master the use of these forms.

As we have already mentioned, the apparently odd behavior of stress in these forms has been explained through the consideration of *–i–* as extrametrical (Harris, 1983), which is therefore not visible for the rules of stress assignment. The notion of extrametricality is none other than the constraint that these forms appear at the end of their base forms and only specifications for gender and number can appear after them, much in the same way as the diminutives, the only difference being that diminutives attach themselves to lexemes and stress assignment still needs to move to the last foot of the word in question.

The desire in traditional studies in morphology to determine the original form from which a specific form is derived has created an increasingly high number of bracketing paradoxes. In English it seems very simple to see that *singing* is derived from the verb *to sing*, and that this word has two different semantic and syntactic functions. It acts as a verbal form in *He is singing*, but it is a noun in *His singing is beautiful*. In Spanish we have *el canto* "the singing," *el cantar* 'the singing," and *cantar* "to sing." The fact that these words are related is obvious, but when we have to decide how *el canto* is derived, we can find ourselves in a quandary. We can posit that it is derived from *cantar* by a regular noun-forming process of adding an article to a verb form. This article can be feminine or masculine, as shown by *el canto* "singing" and *la compra* "shopping," but we have no way of truly knowing which article is going to surface, much in the same way that we do not know the grammatical gender of a number of words in Spanish. To avoid this, we could say that *el canto* is derived from *el cantar* "singing" by taking the gender information from *el* and regularizing the paradigm by adding *–o* to represent the masculine form. If we do this, we find ourselves with no explanation for *la compra*. We have a form *el comprar*, but we do not have *el compro as a possible noun for this verb. Observe that trying to explain the feminine form in *la compra* by associating the final *–a* in the verb with the feminine gender marker would not work because we could say the same thing for *cantar,* which also has an *–a* as a thematic vowel, but we do not have **la canta* as a possible noun form.

This type of discussion takes us nowhere, and we will go in circles trying to decipher what comes first without finding a reasonable solution. What is clear is that all the forms previously mentioned have a base [cant] or [compr] to which something is added to form a noun. Whether the base form is a noun or verb has no relevance at this point.

A New Look at Diminutives[1]

Diminutive formation has been one of the most studied morphophonological processes in Spanish. Although it looks like an apparently simple process, the interaction of phonology and morphology in this example of inflectional and/or derivational morphology gives us a good insight into the inner workings of word formation, syllable structure, stress assignment, etc.

Harris (1983) considers that the peculiarities shown by the addition of the diminutive affix in Spanish are explained by the fact that this affix is added to the word and not to the stem. He bases this assumption on the behavior of words like *miel* "honey" and other words with alternating diphthongs that form the diminutive based on the word with the diphthong and not on the stem [mel]. This explains why we find *–ie* in unstressed positions in the diminutive forms while they are not found in other derivations, such as *miel–meloso* "honey-honeyed," or *fiesta–festejo* "party-celebration," but compare *fiestero* "party-loving."

There is no argument about *miel* "honey" being a word of Spanish in much the same way that there is no argument about *Carlos* "Charles" being a word as well. Nevertheless, when we look at diminutive formation, the diminutive affix is not added directly to the word *Carlos.* If that were the case, we would have a form like ***Carlosito* when the actual form is *Carlitos* instead. This seems to indicate that the base for diminutive affixation is something like *Carl,* which is not a word in Spanish. Trying to ascertain what is a word is not an easy task, but before we move on we need to review some terminology in order to help clarify some important theoretical points.

A root is defined as the smallest possible component, since it cannot be analyzed into smaller parts. The root of a form like *doctor* "male doctor" would be *doct.* The diminutive suffix cannot be added to this form, as more morphological material is needed to come up with the correct derivation. *Doctor* would be the base for the diminutive form and from this we can get the masculine form, but the base for the feminine would be *doctora* "female doctor," and from here we can only arrive at ***doctorita* as the diminutive, which is clearly incorrect. The standard *doctorcita* is formed from the original word *doctor* without the feminine marker. It seems that the diminutive is added to the word, but maybe not the whole word.

Aronoff (1994) defines "stem" as "the phonological domain of a realization rule: that sound form to which a given affix is attached or upon which a given nonaffixal realization rule operates" (39). Without further examination, the stem looks like the base to which the diminutive is added. But in forms like *fiesta-festejo* "party-celebration," a choice needs to be made as to which one of the stems would be used as the base: *fiest–* or *fest–*. It could be argued that these forms have two stems and the one with the diphthong is chosen for the diminutive form, but this decision, although practical, would lack important generalizations.

Aronoff (1994) takes the term "lexeme" from Matthews (1991), who identified three different ways in which the term "word" has been used: sound form (with no relation to meaning), grammatical form, and lexeme. Aronoff (1994) considers the lexeme as being "inherently unspecified for those contextually variable syntactic, semantic, and pragmatically determined categories that are encoded by inflection, although it contains within itself sufficient information for realizing these categories morphophonologically" (10). The lexeme, being by definition an abstraction, could not be used by rule and transformation theories as the base for inflectional and derivational processes, but we can say that it is the lexeme that the speaker has in mind when adding suffixes to stems. In this context a lexeme will be defined as an abstract conceptualization of a word with all pertinent syntactic, morphological, and phonological information available, but without any inflections, which in our particular case refer to the actual manifestation of gender and number.

In order to avoid confusion, in this work we will assume that at the morphophonological level, the diminutive affixes are added to the prosodic word minus all inflection. This includes all class markers. For the purposes of this work, "prosodic word" is defined following Nespor and Vogel (1986) and Goldsmith (1990) as that entity which includes the sound form of a word and all its phonological specifications. If we follow traditional studies, such as Bloomfield (1933), and consider a word as a free form, *Carl*, the apparent base for *Carlitos*, "Charley, Chuck," is not a free form in Spanish in much the same way that *cas*, the base for *casita* "small house" is not a free form either. With this in mind, we can say that the word minus inflection and/or class markers is not a free form, and therefore it is not a word according to the traditional definition. In this sense, this concept of word minus inflection is closer to the definition of the lexeme, and it is in this context that this chapter should be read.

The Formation of the Diminutive: General Description of the Process

The morphological process of diminutive formation is acquired very early in the process of language learning. The subject in López Ornat's study has complete control of this process by age 1:07, exemplified by forms such as **apiita* (*tapita* "small lid"), **etita* (*tetita* "small breast"), and **quitín* (*chiquitín* "male little one"). By age 1:10, we find **Teíto* (diminutive of *Teo*, proper name Theo), **potito* for the diminutive of *poquito* "little bit," and, interestingly enough, we find also *alitas/*alito* for the diminutive of *alas* "wings" and **palito*

Inflection vs. Derivation 73

for the diminutive of *palomitas* "small pidgeons." These examples seem to indicate that diminutive affixation is set in the language learning process even before complete control of grammatical gender.

In order to avoid repetition, we will state the following general characteristics of diminutive formation:

1. Main stress falls invariably on the *–i–* of the affix following the general tendency of Spanish to have binary trochaic feet: align right-and left-headed. This will affect the interaction of vowels in contact: *riíto* small river" not **ríto, *papaíto* or *papacito* "daddy" not **papáito, *rubiecito* or *rubito* "small blond male" not **rubiíto, etc.

2. If the word has a class marker, it is removed and re-attached at the end of the word after the affix has been added: *casa–casita* "small house." No repetition of the same class marker is allowed: *casita* not **casasita.

3. Regardless of the presence or absence of a final vowel in the original word, the diminutive form will have a vowel at the end, followed in some instances by *–s*. It is very rare to have any other consonants at the end of a diminutive form.

4. The productive form of the diminutive affix will always appear at the end of the prosodic word. This is true regardless of how many morphemes have been added to the word: *casa–casita* "house-small house," *casero–caserito* "landlord-small landlord," *caserío–caseriíto* "hamlet-small hamlet," *pan–pancito* "bread-small bread," *panadero–panaderito* "bread maker-small bread maker," *panadería–panaderiíta* "bread shop-small bread shop,"[2] or of the presence of more than one prosodic word. If a structure form with the *mente* suffix were to be used with the diminutive, the suffix would come in between the word and *mente*: *igualmente–***igualicitamente.[3]

Specific Descriptions of Surface Representations

Let us turn now to the specifics of the surface representations of the diminutive:

Polisyllabic words

Words with an unstressed class marker *–a* or *–o*, add *–it*: *casa–casita* "house," *libro–librito* "book," *carro–carrito* "car," *mesa–mesita* "table."

Words that end in unstressed *–e* have two possible outputs:

1) If *–e* acts as a class marker, *-it* is attached to the base without the class marker, and either *–a* or *–o* is attached at the right edge of the affix: *estuche–estuchito* "case," *estudiante–estudiantito(a)* "student," *envase–envasito* "container," *presidente–presidentito(a)* "president."[4]

2) If *–e* is considered part of the base and not a class marker, *-it* is attached to the whole base and a consonant *–c–* (pronounced [θ] or [s] depending on the dialect) is inserted between the *–e* and the *–it* in order to keep the CV sequence: *madre–madrecita* "mother," *padre–padrecito* "father," *clase–clasecita* "class."

Words in (2) can switch to (1), as shown by expressions such as *–¡Ay mi madrita!* "good heavens" and forms such as *compadrito* "godfather" and *comadrita* "godmother."

Words that end in a stressed vowel have several possible outputs:

1) If the final vowel is *–é, –í,* or *–ú,* it is treated as part of the base, and *–it* is attached to it. In order to keep the CV sequence, *–c–* is inserted in between *–é* and *–it–*. An *–a* or *–o* is added at the right edge of the affix according to the gender of the base: *café–cafecito, canapé–canapecito, rubí–rubicito, Perú–Perucito.*

2) Words ending in stressed *–á* follow the same procedure stated in (1), but some speakers: a) attach the affix without insertion of the consonant *–c–*: *papá–papaíto* "dad–daddy, " *mamá–mamaíta* "mom–mommy," José-Joseíto "*Joseph–Joey*"; b) Eliminate the final stressed vowel and attach the affix directly to the base: *papá–papito* "dad–daddy," *mamá–mamita* "mom–mommy."

Words that end in a diphthong have two possible outputs:

1) They add the affix to the last vowel of the base (the word without the class marker *–a, –o*), leaving the vowel of the affix in contact with the vowel of the base. To resolve the group of two identical vowels (one unstressed, one stressed) together, an epenthetic *–e–* is inserted, resulting in three vowels in contact: *–iei–*. To resolve this group, a *–c–* is inserted in between the epenthetic *–e–* and the *–i–* of the affix: *tapia–tapiecita* "adobe or brick wall or fence," *Sonia–Soniecita* "Sonia," *sepia–sepiecita* "sepia, cuttlefish," *sabio–sabiecito* "wise man," *rubio–rubiecito* "male blond."

2) There is a certain amount of variation on these forms, and sometimes the diminutive affix is added directly to the whole form: *Sonia–Sonita* "Sonia," *sabio–sabito* "wise man," *rubio–rubito* "blond man."

Observe that the word *despacio* "slow" has *despacito* as the standard diminutive, and no variation is present for this form. Probably the presence of a *–c–* in the base of this form prevents its re-duplication in the hypothetical **despaciecito.

Words that end in a glide *–y* [j] attach the affix to the base, resulting in the glide-vowel group [ji]. An epenthetic *–e–* is added to break this group: [-jei]. In order to resolve the multi-vowel group and to maximize the onset creating CV groups, a consonant sound [y] is developed and a *–c–* is added to the final form: *rey–reyecito* "king," *ley–leyecita* "law," *buey–bueyecito* "ox." There is no variation on this group, and forms such as: ***reyito,* **leyita are not encountered.

Words with alternating diphthongs on the penultimate syllable attach the affix to the base adding *–e–* and *–c–*: *bueno–buenecito* "good," *piedra–piedrecita* "stone," *fiesta–fiestecita* "party." This choice is typical of peninsular Spanish. Or they attach the affix to the base without any extra additions. This choice is typically associated with Latin American Spanish: *bueno–buenito, piedra–piedrita, fiesta–fiestita.*

Words ending in consonant *–r* or *–n*:

1) Attach *–it* and insert *–c* to keep the *–r* or *–n* in the syllable before the affix (in this case the coda) much in the same way as forms in (4.a). This

similarity reflects the need to keep the last element of the base in the output: *calor–calorcito, dolor–dolorcito, camión–camioncito, salón–saloncito, pantalón–pantaloncito.*[5]

2) If there is a masculine-feminine pair of the type *pintor–pintora,* the affix is added directly to the stem sans class marker, as usual. Notice that the diminutive of *señora* is *señorcita* and not *señorita.* The latter has been lexicalized to mean "ummarried woman" and therefore is formed like words in 1). The form used to address a married woman in an affective way is *señorcita,* the feminine pair of *señor.*

Words ending in *–s:*

1) If the *–s* is the plural morpheme, it is reattached at the end after the class marker. Diminutive formation proceeds according to the structure of the base: *casas–casitas* "houses," *pantalones–pantaloncitos* "pants," *dientes–dientecitos–dientitos* "teeth."

2) If the *–s* is identified as belonging to the base, not a class marker, *–it* is added directly to the word: *francés–francesito(a)* "French man/woman," *lunes–lunesito*[6] "Monday," *después–despuesito* "after."

3) If the ending is identified as a class marker: a) The diminutive affix is added to what is considered to be the stem, and the class marker is re-attached at the right edge of the affix. These examples have been considered as examples of infixation in Spanish: *Lucas–Luquitas* "Luke," *Carlos–Carlitos* "Charles," *lejos–lejitos* "far away," *azúcar–azuquitar*[7] "sugar." b) The class marker is eliminated completely and the affix is added to what is considered to be the stem: *dosis–dosicita (dosecita, dosita?), tesis–tesicita (tesita?).*[8]

These forms are problematic for native speakers and learners alike, and the tendency is to express the affective meaning by other means: *una pequeña dosis, una breve tesis,* etc.

Words ending in other consonants: Add *–it* directly to the stem. This has the added effect of moving a consonant that was originally in the rhyme to the onset of the newly stressed syllable. This process is an example of the maintenance of the CV syllable structure. Compare these forms to the ones ending in a glide *–y*: *lapiz–lapicito,*[9] *verdad–verdadita, reloj–relojito, papel–papelito.*

Monosyllabic Words

These have two possible outputs: 1) Add *–e* and *–c–*: *mal–malecito, mar–marecito(a), pan–panecito, cal–calecita.* 2) Add only *–c–*: *mal–malcito, mar–marcito(a), pan–pancito, cal–calcita.* From the previous data, we can make the following generalizations:

1) The phonological, prosodic, and morphological structure of the base affects the output.

2) The original CV structure must be preserved.

3) The general tendency of the diminutive is to have an *–a* or an *–o* as final vowel followed by the plural morpheme, if there is one. The only exceptions are

cases like *Victor–Victitor* "Victor" and *azúcar–azuquitar* "sugar," where *–or* and *–ar* are interpreted as class markers and therefore get extracted and then reattached at the right edge of the word.

4) Diminutive formation is a process by which, without exception, a left-headed binary foot is created at the end of the affected form. This process takes place with minimal interference from the syllabic structure and phonetic specifications of the form it is applied to. This attachment gives rise to some give and take between representations already in place and some new representations created by the attachment itself.

An Optimality Theory View of Diminutive Formation

The previous sections gave us pertinent and relevant information about the diminutive process, but unfortunately it has not given us a clear view of the processes at hand. In order to attempt to give a better description of the principles at work in processes like diminutive formation, we will now move on to an OT analysis of this process.

The following constraints play a role in this process one way or another. As we analyze the different forms, only those constraints relevant to the form studied will be used in the tables, but reference to other constraints will be made whenever necessary. As customary in OT, the pointing hand signals the winning candidate.

    1. MAXIO (IO): Maximize Input Output. Every element in the input has a representation in the output.
    2. ONSET: Syllables have onsets.
    3. *CODA: Syllables have no coda.
    4. MAXIOSYLL (MIOS): Every element of the structure of the syllable in the input must have a representation in the output.
    5. *REPEAT (R): No segment or morpheme is repeated.
    6. RECOVERY (REC): No opacity allowed. The input ought to be recoverable from the output.
    7. FOOTBINARY (FB): Feet are binary.
    8. ALIGNR: Feet align with the right edge of the word.
    9. HEADLEFT: (HL) Feet are left-headed (strong-weak).

Table 7.1. Possible Rankings for *mesa* "table" (fem.)

me.sV+dim+V	*R	REC	IO	ONSET	ALIGNR	FB
a. me.sa.í.ta	*	*		*		
b. me.sa.cí.ta	*	*	*			
c. me.sa.e.cí.ta	*	*	**	*		
☞d. me.sí.ta			*			
e. me.sái.ta	*	*			*	*

In Table 7.1, (d) emerges as the winner even though it violates MAXIO. (a), (b), (c), and (e) all violate *REPEAT; they keep two copies of the feminine

Inflection vs. Derivation

gender morpheme, when only one is needed at the right edge of the word. (a), (b), (c), and (e) also violate REC. It is not clear yet which of these two constraints is ranked higher. A broken line is used to signify that these two constraints are as yet unranked with respect to each other. They are ranked in relation to the other constraints.

Table 7.2. Possible Rankings for *calor* "heat" (masc.)

ca.lor+dim+V	REC	MIOS	*R	IO	*CODA
a. ca.lo.rí.to	*!	*!			
☞ b. ca.lor.cí.to				*	*
c. ca.lo.ro.cí.to	*!	*	*	**	
d. ca.lo.re.cí.to	*	*		**	

In Table 7.2, there are two candidates with two constraint violations, but (a) has two fatal violations, as its syllabic structure does not contribute to recoverability. We do not know if the base form was *calor* "heat" or a hypothetical form like **caloro/calorro* or **calore/calorre*. The status of final *–r* in Spanish makes it impossible to discriminate if the segment is /r/ or /rr/, therefore re-syllabification is not allowed by REC.[10] (b) emerges as the winner even though it adds an extra segment and has a coda, therefore violating IO and *CODA. It is not clear whether REC or MIOS is the higher-ranked in this table, but since they both have the same violations, we would consider REC to be the higher-ranked constraint in this instance.

Table 7.3. Possible Rankings for *papel* "paper" (masc.)

pa.pel+dim+V	REC	IO	ONSET	*CODA
a. pa.pel.cí.to		*		*
b. pa.pe.le.cí.to	*	**		
c. pa.pe.le.í.to	*	*	*	
☞ d. pa.pe.lí.to				

Words ending in *–l* have always been a problem when explaining the diminutive forms, as it was not clear why these forms did not behave like other words ending in consonants, like the ones analyzed on pp. 74-75 above. Looking at table 7.3, we can see what always seemed somewhat natural: (d) emerges as the winning candidate because it proves to be optimal by not violating any of the high-ranked constraints. Contrary to what happens to *–n* and *–r* in final or coda position, there is no constraint against *–l* re-syllabifying in this position. Words ending in *–l* do not violate REC, although they do violate MIOS. This is one more sign that REC is the higher-ranked constraint in Spanish.

Table 7.4. Possible Rankings for *madre* "mother" (fem.)

ma.dre+dim+V	Rec	Onset	IO
☞a. ma.dre.cí.ta			*
b. ma.dre.í.ta		*!	
c. ma.drí.ta	*!		*

In Table 7.4, (c) fails because of a fatal violation to Rec. Because the *–e* of the base is not kept, there is no way of knowing what the original form was. The lack of onset in (b) becomes a fatal violation because by leaving *–ei–* in contact without an intervening consonant would eventually cause a stress shift from the *–í* to the *–e*. This movement is characteristic of Spanish, where the open vowel becomes the syllabic nucleus and the high vowel becomes a glide, as we can see in words like *peine* "comb" [péj.ne]. This change in a form like ***madreíta-madréita* would make this word impossible to recognize as a diminutive.

Table 7.5. Possible Rankings for *camión* "truck" (masc.)

ca.mión+dim+V	Rec	MIOS	IO	*Coda
a. ca.mio.ní.to	*	*		
☞b. ca.mion.cí.to			*	*
c. ca.mio.ne.cí.to	*	*	**	

In Table 7.5, (b) surfaces as the winner since it is the only candidate that maintains the same original syllable structure retaining the *–n* in coda position. It does this by violating IO and *Coda. (a), although it satisfies IO and *Coda, cannot be the winning candidate thanks to the special status of *–n* in final or coda position. In terms of recoverability, the system has no way to discriminate between all the possible realizations of this segment in final position [N, n, ŋ, m, etc.]. In view of this, re-syllabification of this segment in this position is prevented from happening by Rec and MIOS.

Table 7.6. Possible Rankings for *lápiz* "pencil" (masc.)

lá.piz+dim+V	IO	Rec	*R	MIOS	Onset	*Coda
a. la.pi.í.to	*	*	*	*	*	
☞b. la.pi.cí.to				*		
c. la.pi.to	*	*		*		
d. la.pi.ce.cí.to	**!	*		*		
e. la-piz.cí.to	*		*			*

Table 7.6 gives us a rare opportunity to see different parts of Spanish morphophonology acting in unison. In (a), the final *–z* is not present, therefore violating IO. The missing *z* in (a) leaves two similar vowels together in two different syllables. The stressed *–í* is the head of an onsetless syllable. (c) could be the resolution of the problems incurred by (a), but it violates IO. (d) has two

fatal violations of IO, and (e), although it does not violate the high-ranked MIOS, violates IO by introducing a –c– not present in the input. It also violates *R by having two [θ] (or [s], depending on the dialect) segments together.[11] (b) emerges as the winner because it is the only candidate that does not violate IO, REC and *R. Much in the same way as in cases like *papel-papelito*, (b) wins because it does not violate any of the higher-ranked constraints, given that there is no restriction for the re-syllabification of this form.

One interesting observation is the role that the Obligatory Contour Principle, here represented by *R, plays in the output versions of these forms. (e) does not surface as the output because it violates a high-ranked constraint avoiding repetition of similar sounds in the segmental string. This is a phonological constraint brought to bear on this issue by the addition of a morpho-lexical element represented by the diminutive morpheme in this case.

Table 7.6 indicates that IO and *R seem to work together as a type of conjunct constraint. In this case, the candidate with no violations of either IO and *R seems to win over all others.

It is also worthwhile to mention the curious role of MIOS in these cases. At first glance, it seems to be a very high-ranked constraint, since it is violated by all but one candidate. This would tend to indicate the promotion of this constraint as the one that chooses the winning candidate: (e). But as it was just explained, this particular candidate fails to prevail due to its violation of IO and *R.

Table 7.7. Possible Rankings for *río* "river" (masc.)

ri.V+dim+V	IO	REC	*R	ONSET
a. ri.to	*	*		
☞ b ri.í.to			*	*
c. rie.cí.to	**!		*	

In Table 7.7, (a) violates the constraints MAXIO and REC because it eliminates one of the vowels, thereby making this form unrecoverable, since it now has the same form as the word *rito* "rite." In most cases when the diminutive is added, the word syllable count increases at least by one, and **rito* as a possible diminutive of *río* maintains the same number of syllables as the form without the affix. Note that the diminutive of the word *rito* "rite" would be *ritito*. (b) has two similar vowels, but they belong to two different morphemes, one to the base and the other to the diminutive affix. If the OCP or *R, as we call it here, were allowed to win, there would be no way to recuperate the original form, since it would be confused with *rito* "rite."

Table 7.8. Possible Rankings for *leona* "lioness" (fem.)

le.on+dim+V	MIOS	IO	*CODA
a. le.o.ní.ta	*		
☞b. le.on.cí.ta		*	*
c. le.o.ne.cí.ta	*	**!	

In this case we would expect that **leonita* would be the winning candidate, but instead *leoncita,* which violates IO, ends up being the winner. The fact that this is the feminine form of a masculine word ending in *–n*: *león* "lion" plays an important role here. Also, information about the morphological structure of these forms is of importance in these formations. When the speaker does not relate the suffix *–on* with an augmentative form and there is not an equivalent masculine form, words ending in *–ona* behave exactly as expected. See, for instance, *persona–personita* "person," *acetona–acetonita* "acetona," *Pamplona–Pamplonita* "Pamplona."[12] This is just one more example of how important it is to take morphological information into account when looking at the phonological realization of inflected forms. Pairs like *peatón–peatona* "male–female pedestrian," *león–leona* "lion-lioness," *llorón–llorona* "male-female person given to weeping" need to be related when adding the diminutive affix. The same is true for pairs such as *doctor–doctorcito* "male doctor," *doctora–doctorcita* "female doctor." This fact supports our claim that the diminutive is not added to the word, if we define word as a free form with gender and inflection already assigned. It is added instead to a lexeme with all the information needed but not actually specified or realized before the addition of the affix. Representations such as *doctor* and *llorón* are the base for both masculine and feminine forms of the diminutive. The gender morpheme is added or specified after diminutive affixation.

Table 7.9. Possible Rankings for *tapia* "stone (adobe, mud, etc.) decorative and/or protective outside wall or fence" (fem.)

tá.piV+dim+V	MIOS	*R	REC	ONSET	IO
a. ta.pi.í.ta	*	*	*	*	*
b. ta.pí.ta	*		*		*
c. ta.pie.í.ta			*!		*
☞d. ta.pie.cí.ta					**
e. ta.pi.cí.ta	*		*		*
f. ta.pia.í.ta		*		*	
g. ta.pia.cí.ta		*			*

We have chosen to include a good number of different candidates in Table 9 in order to highlight the interactions between vowels and vocoids in Spanish. Vowels are defined as vocalic segments that can be the nucleus of the syllable; that is, they can carry stress. Vocoids are defined as vocalic segments that can-

Inflection vs. Derivation 81

not be the nucleus of the syllable and therefore cannot carry stress. The form *tapia* has two vowels and one vocoid. The first vowel, –*a*–, carries the main stress; the second –*a* does not carry the main stress, but it is the nucleus of its own syllable by being the most sonorous segment in the syllable –*pia*–. The –*i* is a vocoid and as such cannot carry the stress or be the nucleus. In (a), –*i*– is by itself in its own syllable and functions as the nucleus, and it could carry the stress, but this violates MIOS, which requires that syllables maintain their structure. In other words, what was once a vocoid cannot be changed into a vowel. Notice that (a) violates a number of other constraints as well. It violates *R by having two forms of the same vocalic segment next to each other. It violates REC as it is not possible to recuperate the original input from this form. Since the original vocoid is now represented as a vowel, the speaker has no alternative but to look for a vowel in the original form, and in doing so, would come up with a hypothetical form close to **tapía, following the same pattern as in *río*.

(b) violates MIOS for the same reasons mentioned for (a). It also violates REC by having the same diminutive form as *tapa–tapita* "lid." (c) and (d) both violate IO by introducing segments not present in the input, but (c) also violates ONSET. (d) emerges as the winning candidate by not violating any of the higher-ranked constraints, although it does so by violating IO twice. (e) fails by violating MIOS and REC, while (d) and (f) fail by repeating the terminal gender vowel, which is not allowed by *R.

It is important to add that if (c) and (f) were chosen as the winning candidates, they would surface as **tapiéita and **tapiáita by a general constraint which requires that the most sonorous segment in the syllable be the nucleus. –*e*– and –*a*–, being more sonorous than –*i*– in the sonority scale, would eventually attract the main stress for these forms. Notice also that if –*i*– were to remain a vowel, it would conflict with the constraints FB and HEADLEFT.

Table 7.10. Possible Rankings for *rey* "king" (masc.)

rey+dim+V	FB	ONSET	*R	MIOS	IO
a. re.í.to	*	*		*	*
b. rei.í.to	*	*	*		
c. re.yí.to	*			*	*
d. re.ye.í.to		*		*	*
☞e. re.ye.cí.to				*	**
f. rei.cí.to	*				*

Rey is a monosyllabic word that ends in two vocalic segments, a vowel and a vocoid. Words with at least one binary foot, such as *casa* "house," *libro* "book," etc., with the addition of the diminutive suffix, add one extra syllable for a total of three syllables. Table 7.11 shows these structures.

Table 7.11. Foot and Syllable Structure: *casa–casita*[13]

a.
```
     O  N   O  N
     |  |   |  |
    (c  a   s  a)
     \ /   \ /
      σ     σ
      |     |
      s     w
       \   /
         s
```

b.
```
     O  N    O  N   O  N
     |  |    |  |   |  |
     c  a   (s  i   t  a)
     \ /    \ /    \ /
      σ      σ      σ
      |      |      |
      w      s      w
              \    /
                s
```

In forms such as these, after the diminutive is added we have a left-headed binary foot at the right edge of the word and a stray weak foot at the left edge of the word. This is a standard construction in Spanish as long as the original form in question has at least one binary foot previous to inflection.

In monosyllabic forms, there seems to be a constraint against stray feet, and therefore all-inclusive binary feet need to be constructed when adding the diminutive to these forms. This is similar to what Antilla and Cho (1998) found for Finnish, where odd and even number syllables are inflected differently and morphology reflects the alternation between stressed and unstressed syllables.

There is also a universal constraint against the presence in the output of similar or equal contiguous segments. One of the manifestations of this constraint is the one we represent here as *R (NOREPEAT). When the diminutive is added to *rey* we end up with the form [[[rei]it]o], which becomes [[rei.i.t]o], where we have three vocalic segments together, one of them with no onset, to make the most common syllable form in Spanish: CV. The repair strategy applied here requires the development of a consonantal segment [y] to maximize the onset and to avoid the presence of three vocalic segments next to each other. The resulting hypothetical form would be **reyito*, but this form conflicts with the constraint prohibiting the presence of non-binary feet, and to avoid this, an epenthetic *e* is introduced in between the –*y*– and the –*i*–: **reyeito*. But this last form still leaves us with an onsetless syllable, and as a repair strategy, a –*c*– gets inserted in between the –*e*– and the –*i*–: *reyecito*. It is important to mention here that an alternate form, such as *reicito*, is not completely disallowed by native speakers, which seems to indicate that the constraint against similar segments is ranked higher than the one against non-binary feet. We could also think of a possible syllabic structure *re.i.ci.to* which would preserve the two binary feet for those speakers who consider this form possible, but we would still have an onsetless syllable. For the purposes of this study, nothing crucial hinges on either of these explanations, although it would be interesting to explore these cases further.

Table 7.12. Possible Rankings for *reina* "queen" (fem.)

rei.nV+dim+V	ONSET	*R	REC	IO
a. rei.na.í.ta	*	*		
☞b. rei-ní.ta				*
c. rei.ne.cí.ta			*	**

Note in Table 7.12 that the issues raised in the previous form *rey* do not arise here because *reina* has a clear onset *–n–* in its second syllable and an original binary foot. We can see that it is the interaction of constraints such as ONSET, *R, and REC, together with ALIGNRIGHT, FB, and HEADLEFT, which decides the final output in Spanish. (a) fails because it violates ONSET and *R. (c) fails as well because it would be very difficult to recuperate the original form. This leaves (b) as the optimal candidate.

Table 7.13. Possible Rankings for *bueno* "good" (adj.) (masc.)

bue.nV+dim+V	FB	*R	ONSET	IO	*CODA
a. bue.no.í.to		*	*		
b. bue.ní.to	*			*	
☞c. bue.ne.cí.to				**	
d. bue.no.cí.to		*		*	
e. buen.cí.to	*				*

In Table 7.13 there is the possibility of having two different inputs. One would be to use the form *buen* as the base for the masculine and feminine forms, much in the same way as in *doctor–doctorcito–doctorcita*. The other would be to consider *buenV* as the base. If the base form is *buen*, according to what we said previously for Table 7.12, we need to have two binary feet as the output. If the base is *buenV*, we already have a binary foot in the original form, and therefore we can add *–it–* without further adjustments. (c) surfaces as the winner, even though it violates IO twice, because it satisfies the higher-ranked FB.

We could also say that the base form for the dialects that say *buenito* is *bu.e.n*, which would satisfy FB, but not ONSET; while the base form for dialects that say *buenecito* would be *buen*, which would need to violate IO twice in order to satisfy FB and ONSET. If we compare these forms with forms such as *abuelo*, which also have *–ue–*, we can conclude that the base form for the latter has to be *a.bue.lV*, and not *a.bu.e.lV*, as we do not have **abuelecito as a possible output.

84   Inflection vs. Derivation

Table 7.14. Possible Rankings for *piedra* "stone" (fem.)

pie.drV+dim+V	FB	*R	Onset	Rec	IO
a. pie.dra.í.ta		*	*		
b. pie.dra.cí.ta		*		*	*
c. pe.drí.ta	*			*	*
☞d. pie.dre.cí.ta				*	**
e. pie.dre.í.ta			*	*	*
f. pie.dri.ta	*				*
g. pi.e.drí.ta			*		*

In Table 7.14, (d) emerges as the winning candidate if FB has a higher ranking. If this constraint were not ranked higher, (g) would surface as the winning candidate. Notice also that this last candidate satisfies REC, while (d) does not. Forms with stem alternating dipthongs such as *piedra–pedrada* "stone–blow with/from a stone," *puerto–portuario* "port–pertaining to a port," *hierba–herbolario* "grass–herbalist/herborist," *muerto–mortuario* "dead–mortuary," *mueble–mobiliario* "piece of furniture–furnishings," etc. have a diphthong *–ie/ue* in stressed position and a simple vowel *–e/o* in unstressed position in processes usually associated with derivational morphology in nouns and with special conjugations in verbs. In *piedra*, *–ie* carries the stress (piédra), but the first *–e–* in *pedrada* is now stressless, as the stress falls in the first *–a–* (pedráda).

Alternating diphthongs in noun and verb morphology have been the subject of countless studies in Spanish. They are especially interesting in diminutive formation because, contrary to what could be expected, we do not find a simple vowel on the diminutive form. We find a diphthong instead, although that position is now clearly unstressed, as the stress falls without exception on the *–i–* of the diminutive suffix. This fact is what made scholars like Harris (1983) and others conclude that diminutive formation operated at the word level. One other interesting occurrence in these forms is that words with alternating diphthongs have what native speakers consider to be two different possible forms for the diminutive. These forms are currently associated with specific dialects of Spanish, but speakers from all varieties—although they themselves favor one over the other—all consider both possible. According to this, forms such as *piedra* have two different possible diminutives: *piedrita* and *piedrecita*. The former is currently being favored by speakers of Latin American Spanish, the latter by speakers of Peninsular Spanish. As we mentioned before, the constraint FOOTBINARY requires that feet be binary in Spanish. So far we have seen that it can be satisfied by having a binary foot in the original word (*casa–casita*) or by requiring that all feet be binary (*bueno–buenecito, pie–piececito*). For the purposes of this analysis, we will consider FOOTBINARY as one constraint but allow it to have two rankings: the regular ranking, which is required in forms with an original binary foot, and what we would call the strong ranking, which is required in monosyllabic forms and in forms with alternating diphthongs. This is similar to what Antilla and Cho (1998) called "partial rule ordering."

This long disquisition allows us to explain forms like *piedra–piedrita–piedrecita* within an OT theory of ranked violable constraints. For the dialect group that favors *piedrecita*, the ranking of FOOTBINARY is very high, while in the dialects favoring *piedrita*, this constraint has a lower ranking. The question that immediately comes to mind is why this should be the case. We do not have an exact answer for this question at the moment, and we will have to leave this subject open for further study. It is very interesting indeed that this alternation exists precisely in forms where we have alternating diphthongs in the base form and in some monosyllabic words, but not in other forms. It seems like the interpretation of the diphthong as mono-moraic or bi-moraic plays a role in this variation.

For comparison purposes, we will now look at a form that has a non-alternating rising diphthong.

Table 7.15. Possible Rankings for *piano* "piano" (masc.)

pia.nV+dim+V	REC	*R	ONSET	FB	IO	MIOS
a. pia.no.í.to	*	*	*			
☞b. pia.ní.to				*	*	
c. pi.a.ní.to			*		*	*
d. pia.no.cí.to	*	*			*	
e. pia.ne.cí.to	*				**	
f. pia.ne.í.to	*		*			*

In Table 7.15, the winning candidate is chosen by a ranking of REC>*R>ONSET. (c) is given only as an illustration of how these forms are excluded from the output. In Table 7.14, the winning candidate was selected from a ranking of FB>*R>ONSET. In order to meet the requirements of FB, REC gets demoted below ONSET in Table 7.14, while REC remains the highest ranked constraint in Table 7.15. Note that so far the only winning candidates that violate IO—sometimes twice—are those that do not violate another high-ranked constraint.

Table 7.16. Possible Rankings for *mal* "evil" (masc.)

mal+dim+V	FB	ONSET	*CODA	REC	MIOS	IO
a. ma.lí.to	*			*	*	
☞b.ma.le.cí.to				*	*	**
c. mal.cí.to	*		*			*
d. ma.le.í.to		*		*	*	*

Once again in Table 7.16 we can see the effect of a high-ranked FOOTBINARY. It eliminates (a), which is also eliminated by REC, as there is no way to recuperate the original form from (a). As it is, (a) would be associated with the adjective *malo* "bad" and not with the noun *mal* "evil."

Table 7.17. Possible Rankings for *malo* "bad" (masc.)

ma.lV+dim+V	REC	ONSET	*CODA	IO
a. ma.le.cí.to	*			**
☞b. ma.lí.to				*
c. ma.le.í.to	*	*		*
d. mal.cí.to			*	*

In Table 7.17, (a) is not the successful candidate in this case because it fails REC. (d), although it fails *CODA and IO in this table and failed FOOTBINARY in Table 7.16, is the candidate chosen for some speakers when attempting to make the diminutive of Table 7.16, while no speaker selects it as a possible output for *malo* "bad." The winning candidate for this form is (b). It would be tempting to associate forms such as *mal* with forms such as *doctor–doctorcito(a), llorón–lloróncito(a)*, but we have to keep in mind that the former are both nouns. While *mal* is a noun, *malo* is an adjective. We can say that *malo(a)* is derived from *mal* by gender specification. Once this is done, the input form for diminutive addition is [*malV*] for *malo(a)* and [mal] for *mal*.[14]

There is a small but pervasive group of Spanish words that have as a terminal element something other than the vowels –*o* or –*a*. Forms such as *Victor–Victitor, Carlos–Carlitos*, etc. have been explained as an example of an infix in Spanish (Jaeggli, 1981), but although this explanation describes diminutive formation for these forms, it does not help us to explain the process at hand. In this study we will consider the last vowel and consonant of these forms as the terminal marker signifying the end of the word. As such this terminal marker needs to appear at the right edge of the word in the same way the terminal vowel –*a* or –*o* appears at the end of the forms already studied.

Table 7.18. Possible Rankings for *Carlos* "Charles" (masc.)

Car.los+dim+TM	REC	*R	IO	ONSET	*CODA
a. Car.lo.sí.to	*	*	*		*
b. Car.lo.í.to	*	*	*	*	*
c. Car.lo.sí.tos	*	**			**
☞d. Car.lí.tos			*		**
e. Car.lí.to	*		*		*

In Table 7.18, (a) and (c) both fail REC, as they could be reinterpreted as the diminutive of a hypothetical form **Carloso* (a) or **Carlosos* (c). They also fail *R by keeping the –*o* (a) or –*os* (c) of the terminal marker inside and outside of the final form. Additionally, (a) violates IO by not having the –*s* of the terminal marker at the end of the word. (b) fails REC. The missing –*s* makes it impossible to recuperate the original form. It repeats the –*o* of the terminal marker, incurring an *R violation. The missing *–s* makes it violate IO, and it also fails ONSET by having a syllable with just a vowel and no consonantal element. (d) is the winning candidate; it incurs no violations of REC and *R, although it violates IO and *CODA.

We have just seen that not all diminutive forms end in *–a* or *–o*. Although the terminal element in the diminutive serves in most occurrences as the gender marker (*-a* for feminine and *–o* for masculine), this is not the case in all instances. Words like *el mapa* "map," *la mano* "hand," etc., are examples where *–a* and *–o* do not identify gender.

Table 7.19. Possible Rankings for *mapa* "map" (masc.)

ma.pa+dim+V	REC	*R	*CODA	ONSET	IO
☞ a. ma.pí.ta					*
b. map.í.ta			*!	*	*
c. ma.pí.to	*!				**
d. ma.pa.í.ta		*		*	

In Table 7.19, the winning candidate, (a), violates IO but meets all the higher-ranked constraints. (b), included here for demonstration purposes, has a fatal violation of *CODA. It has a voiceless obstruent *–p* in coda position, which is not allowed within the segmental distribution in Spanish. This placement of *p* leaves the next vowel unattached to a consonant, causing (b) to incur an ONSET violation as well. (c) has a fatal violation of REC, since the only possible original form would be **mapo. (d) is a good example of how the only candidate that does not violate IO is prevented from surfacing as the optimal output by a violation of *R, a higher-ranked constraint in Spanish.

Table 7.20. Possible Rankings for *mano* "hand" (fem.)

ma.no+dim+V	*R	REC	ONSET	IO	FB
a. ma.no.í.ta	*		*		
b. ma.no.cí.ta	*	*		*	
c. ma.ní.ta		*		*	*
☞ d. ma.ní.to				*	*

Forms like *mano* present a very interesting case because they actually have two possible outputs for the diminutive: *manita*, recuperating the gender specific *–a*, and *manito*, copying the *–o–* from the original form. The former is characteristic of peninsular varieties, and the latter predominates in Latin American varieties. In Table 7.20, the winning candidate is (d) because it does not violate REC. (c) loses to (d) precisely because it violates REC. For those language varieties where the final vowel of the diminutive must have an unequivocal identification with *–a* (feminine), *–o* (masculine), (c) becomes the winning candidate, even though this form incurs an extra IO violation. The *–o* at the end of *mano* is interpreted as a terminal marker, and as such it must appear at the end of the output. *R does not allow two copies of the terminal element to surface in the output, and therefore (a) is not chosen as the optimal candidate. Note that (b), a candidate that satisfies FOOTBINARY completely, fails to be the winning candidate by failing REC and *R.[15] Cases like *mapa* and *mano* allow us to see why the terminal vowels in these forms must be part of their lexical representation. There is no way to recuperate them otherwise.

So far we have specified the input for diminutive formation in three different ways:

   I. LexemeV+dim+V.
   II. Lexeme+dim+TM.
   III. Lexeme+dim+V.

I. is the base for diminutive formation for those words that have as a terminal element a vowel that corresponds unequivocally to the grammatical gender of the word and identifies it as: *a* (feminine), –*o* (masculine). This vowel is not specified as either –*a* or –*o* at the end of the lexeme, since it will be specified later at the word level. But even though the vocalic terminal element is not specified fully at the end of the lexeme, we still need to have information about the presence of a vowel in that context. As we have seen, it determines the final shape of the diminutive. The presence of this vocalic position is what establishes the existence of a binary foot in most instances. As discussed previously, diminutive affixation behaves differently according to the presence of original binary feet. These forms will always incur in at least one IO violation due to the fact that the V will not be a part of the output in that position. It will be prevented from appearing there by *R, which does not allow the repetition of the same terminal element or morpheme in the output.

II. is the base for diminutive formation for those forms that have more than one segment as a terminal element, usually a vowel and a consonant. Notice that the principle for diminutive formation of these words is the same. The information about TM (terminal marker) is just a device to remind the learning system of the need to add something more than just a vowel at the end of the form.

III. is the base for diminutive formation for words that do not have a vowel at the end of the word that corresponds unequivocally to gender identification –*a* (feminine), –*o* (masculine) as a terminal element. These forms may have a vowel –*e*, –*a*, –*o*, –*i*, –*u* or a consonant at the end. What is important about these forms is that whatever the terminal element may be, it needs to appear in the final output either within the word, or at the end of it: *madre–madrecita, doctor–doctorcito, mapa–mapita, café–cafecito*. If the final vowel of the original word is –*e*, it remains in its original location in the output; if it is –*a* or –*o*, it is interpreted as a type of terminal element and usually gets copied at the end of the output.

Table 7.21. Possible Rankings for *policía* "policeman" (masc.)

po.li.cí.a+dim+V	Rec	MIOS	*R	Onset	IO
☞ a. po.li.ci.í.ta			*	*	*
b. po.li.cí.ta	*	*			**
c. po.li.cia.cí.ta		*	*		*
d. po.li.cie.cí.ta	*				**
e. po.li.ci.í.to	*		*	*	*

Once again we see that forms with stressed vowels in the last syllable do not allow this vowel to be lost or re-syllabified in order to avoid opacity. Rec and MIOS are the higher-ranked constraints producing the winning candidate (a) in Table 7.21. Notice that (e) fails because of a violation of Rec.

Discussion

After looking at how different constraints play a role in the final output for diminutive forms, we have been able to identify several elements that remain constant as well as several elements that stand out as particular to this process.

When deciding what constraints are significant to this process, we must consider the need to have three different constraints that seem to be closely related: IO, MIOS, and Rec. Obviously all of these are somehow related to Faithfulness constraints of the kind postulated in McCarthy (1995), who states that the output must be as close to the input as possible. We would like to divert our attention to determine if the three constraints posited in the present study are legitimate and necessary. The first thing we need to look at is if they can be replaced or included in other already existing constraints.

Previously, in Table 7.2, we saw that Rec and MIOS appeared to have the same ranking in the formation of *calor–calorcito*. Both of these constraints were ranked higher than IO and *Coda. MIOS seems to act as the other side of *Coda. The former requires that the original syllable structure be preserved, even if it means keeping a segment in coda position, while the latter requires syllables not to have Codas. Regardless of these similarities, it is clear that they are two distinct constraints. What we still do not know is if MIOS and Rec are both necessary. In Table 7.3, Rec is ranked higher than MIOS, as the winning candidate in this case violates the latter. In the few cases where *R is violated, MIOS is ranked higher than *R, for example, *policia–policiita*, a case where the two vowels surface in the winning output because the *–i–* of the base has to remain as the nucleus of its own syllable as it was in the original form.

*Repeat is an interesting constraint in that it can be phonology-related when it prevents similar segments from reoccurring, but it can also be morphology-related when it prevents morphemes from being repeated. We have seen its effects in cases like *sabio–sabiecito* (**sabiito*) and *casa–casita* (**casaita* or **casacita*). **sabiito* fails *R because it has two similar segments next to each other, while **casaita* and **casacita* violate *R by repeating the gender morpheme in two different places. Notice that the winning candidates violate IO. This application of *R has far-reaching consequences, as it affects all forms with a gender-specific vowel in final position in its original form before the addition of the diminutive affix. This constraint helps us explain the differences between the outputs of diminutive and plural formations. When forming the diminutive, outputs such as **buenocito are excluded for the same reason a form such as **casasitas is excluded when adding the plural: a violation of *R. The former repeats the terminal element gender marker, while the latter repeats the terminal element plural marker and the gender marker. Nothing needs to be added to *casas* "houses" or *buenos* "good ones" (masc.) when adding the plural because there are no repetitions. It is interesting to note that although forms such as *papases* "fathers" do emerge in some non-standard varieties of Spanish, they have not yet become the standard in any variety, as they violate *R by having the plural morpheme twice in the output. Nevertheless, note that a vowel has been added to this form to avoid a segment repetition: two [s] together would also violate *R. This occurrence gives some insight into the possible prevalence of phonology over morphology in these cases: the repetition of the morpheme is allowed, but not the repetition of the segment [s]. Two [s] segments together would become one, therefore losing information. One possible explanation for cases such as *papases* would be that this form is interpreted as [papás] and it is to this form that the plural morpheme is added. Note that this does not change the role of the *R constraint. It still restricts forms such as [papás]s from surfacing. The winning candidates in this case would be either *papás* or *papases*.

Constraints such as *R do nothing less than blur the boundaries between phonology and morphology even more. A theoretically exclusive decision to avoid mixing of modules would make us eliminate constraints or any type of device that would permit this kind of interleaving effects. One possible solution would be to stipulate two different *R constraints: one restricting morphemes from being repeated (morphology-based) and one restricting segments from being repeated (phonology-based). We had some indication of a higher ranking of the phonology-based constraint in the previous examples. This decision would entail unnecessary repetition, when it is clear that it is the same constraint and it produces the same effects: no repetition of segments and/or morphemes. This is a universal constraint, aimed at the preservation of maximum distinction between contiguous elements, which in turn would aid in maximum comprehension of the speech signal.

In conclusion, the analysis presented here helps explain why final vowels and/or some terminal elements are not kept in the output when new suffixes are added during the process of word formation in Spanish; that is why we do not have forms such as **casaíta or **casaero, but *casita* and *casero*.

By stipulating that the diminutive suffix is added to the lexeme and not to the full word, besides providing a more complete explanation for the process at hand, we also contribute to explaining the different behavior of processes such as the diminutive and the plural in Spanish. The diminutive is added to the lexeme, while the plural is added to the word considered as a free form. The difference between *calor–calorcito* and *calor–calores*—with the final *–r* allowed to re-syllabify in the latter but not in the former—is determined by the incomplete specification of the lexeme, while the word is completely specified and presents no opacity problems.

The Acquisition of Grammatical Gender

Grammatical gender in Spanish is either lexical or syntactic.[16] Lexical gender needs to be learned; syntactic gender requires agreement with some lexical gender already specified. Lexical gender is unpredictable, and although there is a tendency to pair a final *a* with feminine and a final *o* with masculine, there are many exceptions to this.[17] Syntactic gender is completely predictable and there is generally a one-to-one correspondence between *a* for feminine and *o* for masculine. The word *puente* "bridge" has no obvious indication of being grammatically feminine or masculine. It is specified lexically as being masculine in Spanish, thus *el puente*. If we assign an adjective to this word, it will be assigned the gender of the noun it modifies. We can have *el puente alto* "tall bridge," where *alto* has a gender marker *–o* indicating that the adjective refers to a masculine referent, or we can have *el puente grande* "big bridge," where *grande* does not have a clear indication of a specific gender in itself but, in the context of the noun phrase *el puente grande*, the nominalization *el grande* "the big one" can only refer to a masculine referent.

Information about gender is already lexically present when sentences are put together in syntax. At the syntactic level, the specific realization of the gender morpheme or marker will function morphologically as what has been described as "inflection." Gender assignment at the syntactic level does not change the word category, does not affect stress placement, and does not involve major phonological and/or phonetic changes. Gender assignment at this level functions as what used to be called "spell-out rules."

Learning Grammatical Gender in L1

The subject in López Ornat's study has no problem with the acquisition of the gender category when it refers to animate objects as proven by phrases such as **os'tá e miau* for *dónde está el gato* "where is the cat" (masc.), produced at 1:07 years old. As expected, lexical gender is acquired much later. At 1:08 this subject produced **este silla* for *esta silla* "this chair." We cannot say with absolute certainty that this subject does not know that *silla* "chair" is lexically feminine in Spanish at this point, since we did not find other examples with this same word using any other determiners, even in an unanalyzed form. All we can say at this point is that grammatical gender has not been acquired yet. The demonstrative adjective *este* "this" (masc.) is still one unanalyzed lexical item. At 1:10 the subject says **alitas/*alito/*palito* for *palomitas (de maiz)* "popcorn." The fluctuation between *a* and *o* and between *s* and no *s* is a very good example of the non-identification of these endings as morphologically determined to refer to gender and/or number.

By age 2:00, both lexical and grammatical gender seem to have been acquired fully, as indicated by phrases such as *pa abí la perta for para abrir la puerta "in order to open the door." Observe that lexical and grammatical gender are acquired before the acquisition of elements of syllable structure like complex onsets and alternating diphthongs.

Languages in Contact: Giving Spanish Gender to English Words

In order to see how the notions of lexical and grammatical gender are transferred between languages, we conducted a study based on corpus data from taped telephone conversations in Spanish among L1 Spanish speakers living in the U.S. We extracted all instances of English words introduced into the Spanish text, and we looked for information regarding the gender specification given to those words in Spanish. We found 96 instances of English words with a specific reference in Spanish to masculine and feminine gender. There were many instances of English words introduced into the Spanish text, but we are referring here to the ones where information about gender was clearly specified in the text.

Out of the total 96 instances identified, 18 (18.75%) were originally feminine in Spanish but received a masculine gender marker when uttered in English, 58 (60.4%) were originally masculine in Spanish and received a masculine gender marker when uttered in English, and 20 (20.8%) were originally feminine in Spanish and received a feminine gender marker when uttered in English (Table 7.22). In terms of how Spanish gender was assigned to these English words, we found that 81.25% of the English words were assigned the same original gender they had in Spanish, 18.75% changed an original feminine gender to masculine, and 0% changed an original masculine gender to feminine.

Table 7.22. Spanish Gender for English Words

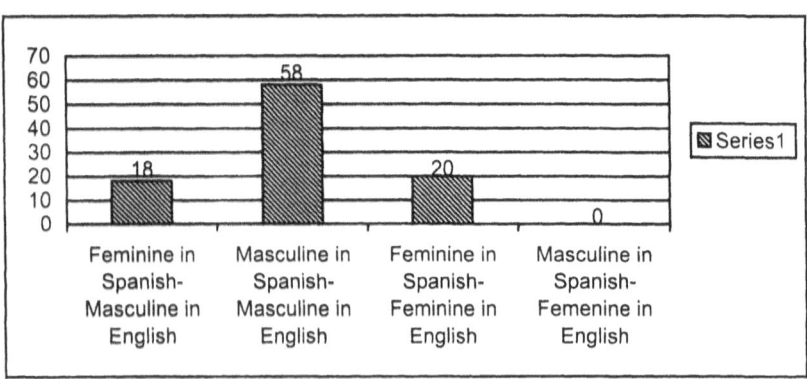

In Table 7.22, we can see that the majority of English words are assigned the same gender classification they had originally in Spanish. This is not surprising. What is surprising is that we did not find any instances of change in gender when the original Spanish word was masculine. This indicates that masculine words generally keep their lexical gender, while feminine words are sometimes changed to masculine. Looking at what kinds of words kept their feminine gender, we found that these words usually designated specific objects and/or places: *una engine, la green card, la Italian House*, while the ones that changed to masculine tended to designate events and/or activities: *el shower* (as in a baby shower), *el open house, el shopping*. We need to mention that this pattern only signals tendencies, since there are examples of all these types in both groups. Consider *el freeway* for *la autopista*.

Table 7.23. Assignment of Spanish Gender to English Words

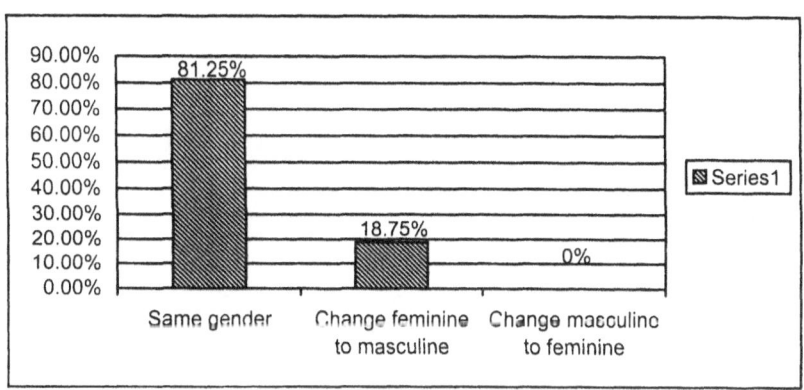

In general, we can say that masculine gender assignment is the most common transfer made in cases where we have an English word within a Spanish context. This seems to corroborate the general notion that the masculine gender is the default gender in Spanish, but when introducing gender to English words, Spanish native speakers also base their decisions on the original gender in Spanish.[18]

Notes

1. There are many areas of study when we look at such rich phenomena as the diminutive. In this chapter we will only look at the productive formation with the morpheme *–it*. We will not look at a semantic explanation of these forms, as this issue will take us too far afield. We must mention that the diminutive adds different meanings to the base to which it is added. These meanings encompass, but are not limited to, smallness and the notion of being a term of endearment and/or scorn, contempt, disdain, etc.

2. This is a natural consequence of the meaning of this affix: speakers do not refer emotionally to only one part of a complex word, but to the whole word itself.

3. Almost any word in Spanish can have the diminutive affix added to it, and speakers often play with all the possibilities. Of course, some of the possibilities will not occur because of morphosyntactic, phonotactics, and/or semantic restrictions.

4. Notice that *envase* and *estuche* will not have a change in gender, while we now have a possible contrast between *el estudiante–la estudiante(a)* and *el presidente–la presidente(a)*.

5. It has been noted by Castro (1998) that in the Canary Islands we encounter examples of *pantalonito*.

6. This form appears sometimes written as *lunecito*. This spelling implies the addition of *–c–* with the subsequent assimilation of the group *–sc–* to *–c–*.

7. We found this example in the data from López Ornat's subject at age 2:08.

8. We are not looking at other forms of the diminutive affix, but in this case it is relevant to compare this form with the existing *tesina* "undergraduate thesis, honor's project," which has been lexicalized to mean a different type of *tesis* "thesis."

9. Notice that the presence of *–z* in *lápiz* and *–c–* in *lapicito* represents only an orthographic convention, as the sound remains the same: [θ] in some varieties of Peninsular Spanish, [s] everywhere else.

10. We use /r/ to represent the segment in *caro* and /rr/ to represent the segment in *carro*.

11. We are using the regular spelling conventions for Spanish, and the written *–z–* and *–c–* represent only orthographic differences. The two symbols represent the same sound in this case.

12. The form *Pamplonica* has been re-lexified to mean a person from Pamplona, not the actual city.

13. "O" stands for "Onset" and "N" for "Nucleus." The symbol σ' represents "syllable," "w" stands for "weak" and "s" for "strong."

14. Notice the difference in meaning between the forms *está mal* "He/she/it is not doing well" and *está malo* "he/she/it/ is sick." Compare this last form with *es malo* "he/she/it/ is bad."

15. The *–o* as a non-gender terminal marker has a special status. Compare *manecillas* "hands" (of a watch), an already lexicalized diminutive form.

16. We are not including here the notion of gender where there is a connection between sex and gender.

17. See Harris (1991) for an excellent study of Spanish noun classes.

18. See Appendix II for a list of examples of grammatical gender transfer taken from the recorded telephone conversation data used in this section.

VIII.
Phonological Processing and Second/Foreign Language Learning Difficulties

Phonemic Awareness and Language Learning Difficulties

Within the field of language acquisition it has been said that learning a second and/or foreign language can be analyzed as a process that: 1) reflects the same procedures as learning a first language, 2) reflects some, but not all, of the same procedures; or 3) is completely different.

Through research in this area, sequenced acquisition stages have been identified where the learner language becomes an interlanguage. At the end of every developmental sequence there is potentially a formally correct target-like production. We have to keep in mind that even though first language acquisition (if all requirements are present) is always successful, second language acquisition encounters variable degrees of success. There are many variables that influence acquisition. Larsen-Freeman and Long (1991) identified six: 1) age, 2) language aptitude, 3) social-psychological factors: motivation and attitude, 4) personality: self-esteem, extroversion, anxiety, risk taking, sensitivity to rejection, empathy, inhibition and tolerance to ambiguity, 5) cognitive style, and 6) learning strategies.

One important factor in second/foreign language acquisition is instruction, which has proven to affect the rate of acquisition, but not necessarily the order of acquisition sequences. Across different languages students seem to acquire the same structures in the same sequence, which appears to resemble principles of Universal Grammar.

When we talk about variable success in foreign language learning, for the most part we are referring to pronunciation (or what is commonly referred to as accent). First language learners do not have an 'accent' (besides readily recognizable regional varieties), while second/foreign language learners have an accent in most cases. The presence of this foreign accent has been related to the age of first contact with L2: the younger the age of study, the more native-like the pronunciation. The older the learner is at the time of first contact, the more recognizable the accent. It seems that age plays a major role in the acquisition of phonology, and it seems to affect, but not as pervasively, other linguistic components such as syntax, lexicon, semantics, etc. This aspect of foreign language learning has been studied as the critical period hypothesis, which establishes the age between 8 months and 6 years as the magical time for first language learning. The existence of a critical period seems to be widely accepted for first language, but this is not necessarily the case for a second language due to the fact that some speakers attain considerably high degrees of native-like pronunciation regardless of the age of exposure. Nevertheless, this is not true for all learners.

The possibility of variable success in foreign/second language learning has been a constant for adult learners. Variation can range from a very slight foreign accent to the inability to function at all in a foreign language environment, specifically in a foreign language class.

Phonemic awareness has been considered the keystone in learning how to read. The meta-linguistic knowledge needed to decipher and decode language needs to be in place for language learning to occur, be it first language learning or second language learning.

Gillam, Hoffman, and van Kleeck (1998) report on results of a study where phonological awareness was found to be heavily dependent on phonological coding abilities. They also found that training in phonological awareness positively affects phonological coding.

Perception and Production in Phonology: The "*Eusebio* Study"

It has been assumed that phonology in the first language determines and permeates the phonology of the second language. According to this assumption, during the beginning stages, foreign language learning is based on the sounds of the native language. Learners determine which sounds correspond to the new language by establishing which ones are similar or different from their L1. As learning progresses it is assumed that learners move away from replicating native language sounds and start to adopt the new language parameters. In this section we are going to refer again to data collected from the "Eusebio" study mentioned in chapter VI. In this study, a group of students enrolled in a first semester Spanish class, and another group of students enrolled in a third-year Spanish class were asked to write a short paragraph dictated to them in Spanish. After writing down what they heard, they were asked to separate the words into syllables and write any accent mark they considered necessary. The original paragraph in the study was larger, but here we will make reference to a few parts only. The purpose of the study was to look at the level of acquisition of syllable structure, stress assignment, and discrimination of specific sounds. Here, we will concentrate on the perception of /b/. The following is one sample sentence from that study: *Si ahora lo tiene tu amigo Eusebio, lo llamaré por teléfono para*

Phonological Processing and Second/Foreign Language Learning Difficulties 97

pedirselo "If now it is in the hands of your friend Eusebio, I will call him to ask him for it."

After the dictation was done, the students were asked the meaning of the word Eusebio, and if they had heard it or seen it in the written form before. 95% of the students in the advanced group reported that although they did not know the form, and they had not seen it before, they were able to see, based on the context and the position of the word in the sentence, that it was a proper noun.[1] 4.7% of students in the advanced group were not able to identify this form as a proper noun. 38% of students in the beginning group were able to identify the form as a proper noun, although they recognized that they had not seen this particular form before. 47% of the students in the lower level group were not able to identify this form as a proper noun.

Results from the Advanced Group

57% of the students in the third year class used either *b* or *v* to represent [β] in the word Eusebio, and 52% used either *d* or *r*.[2] 13% of the students used *b* only and 30% used *v*.

Table 8.1. Pronunciation of Target /b/

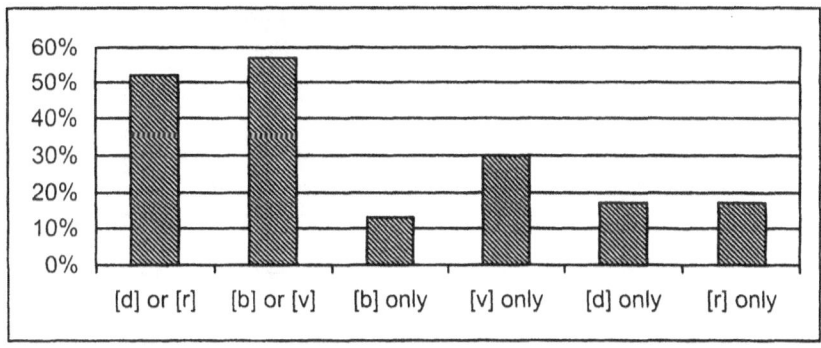

Table 8.2. Forms Encountered in the Third-Year Group

Eu.ce.ri.o (1)[3]	Eusevio (1)	E.ú.se.bio(1)	Eu.sé.di.o(1)
Eus.e.rio (1)	Eusevi.o (1)	Eusebio(1)	e.uce.dio (1)
Eu.se.rio (1)	Eus.e.vi.o (1)	e.uce.bio (1)	eusedio (1)
Eu.ser.i.o (1)	Eu.ce.vi.o (1)		E.u.se.di.o (1)
Eu.se.vio (5)			
Heu.se.vio (1)[4]			
E.o.se.rio (1)	E.u.sa.bio (1)	E.ju.se.dio (1)	
Au.ser.i.o (1)			Teu.ce.dio (1)

It is striking to see the great variety of possible syllabifications chosen by these students. We would expect that by the third year of study, learners ought to show better control of the syllabic structure of Spanish. Of the 66% of students who used [b] or [v], only 38% knew how to separate syllables correctly in Spanish. Of the 26% who used [d], only 16% were able to separate syllables correctly. The students who did not attempt to syllabify the forms were asked the reasons why they did not separate the words in syllables. They expressed that they were unsure about how to do it exactly and chose not to do it. Still, in this group only 11.5% of the instances were left un-syllabified, representing 9.5% of the students in the group. This is in sharp contrast with the results in the beginning group where 71.4% of the students were not able to syllabify, representing 57.6% of the forms produced.

An Attempt at an OT Analysis

We are going to take the forms produced by these students and insert them into an OT Table as possible candidates to see if we can provide some insight into the incipient grammar available to these students at this stage of their learning process. We are not going to examine all the forms produced by the students, instead we will only look at what we consider to be the most representative of their learning state.

Table 8.3. *Eusebio* (masc.) (proper name)

Eu.se.bio	IO	ONSET	*CODA	MIOS
a. Eu.ce.ri.o^5	*	**		*
b. Eus.e.vi.o^6		***	*	**
c. Eu.se.vio				
d. E.ú.se.bio	*	**		*
e. e.uce.bio	*	*		*
f. E.u.se.di.o	***	***		**
g. E.ju.se.dio	***	*		*

These students have acquired a good amount of prosodic information in Spanish. With only one exception (d), they all have identified the stressed syllable correctly. 95% perceived and represented accurately a falling diphthong on the first syllable. 52.3% perceived and represented a rising diphthong in the last syllable, while 38% did not identify these last segments as belonging to a diphthong, and as such, as part of the same syllable. Curiously enough, they all identified the individual specific segments correctly. The latter is true for both groups, which seems to indicate the salience of the end of the word.

In the advanced group all students were able to produce a writing sample of the form pronounced. In the beginning group, 38% of the students were not able to come up with any kind of writing representation for the word *Eusebio*. They were able to write something for some of the other words in the paragraph, but could not even attempt to write Eusebio. They did not identify this form as any recognizable existing word.

Phonological Processing and Second/Foreign Language Learning Difficulties 99

Table 8.4. Syllable Identification

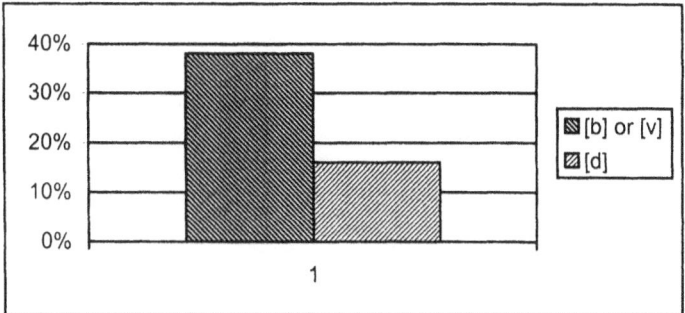

We can see what appears to be at least a weak connection between complete resetting of the phonological parameters and control of syllable structure, although the latter seems to proceed at a much slower pace in the learning system.

Students in the advanced class used for the *Eusebio* study had at least 3 years (most of them more) of formal instruction in Spanish. 9% had spent some time in a Spanish speaking country and 4.7% of these had attended regular school in a Hispanic country.

Different studies have shown that even if at the beginning of foreign language study perception precedes production; it seems that later on students can produce sounds that they did not necessarily perceive correctly. We also have the common effects described as the Conrad syndrome where speakers are able to have excellent control of syntactic and semantic components, but not necessarily show the same level of proficiency in pronunciation.

Table 8.5. Sample Results for [β] in Third-Year Group
(based on number of samples)

Either b and/or v	(4) 15.3%
Only b	(14) 53.8%
Only v	(10) 38.4%
Either d and/or r	(12) 46.1%
Only d	(6) 23.0%
Only r	(6) 23.0%

If we keep in mind that perception implies the use of sensory features, while production implies the use of motor features, we can contrast the sounds the learner perceives:

/b/ = [+labial, +anterior, -coronal, -dental]
[β] = [+labial, +anterior, -coronal, -dental] (allophone in Spanish)
/v/ = [+labial, +anterior, -coronal. +dental] (phoneme in English, allophone in Spanish)
/d/ = [-labial, +anterior, +coronal, +dental]

/r/ = [-labial, +anterior, +coronal, -dental] (phoneme in Spanish, allophone in English [D])

[D] = [-labial, +anterior, +coronal, -dental] English allophone of intervocalic /d/

When choosing a /d/ over a [β] to represent what they heard, these students are choosing [anterior] as the relevant feature, but we must keep in mind that /d/ is used in this context because the student cannot find in his native language a /b/ with a change in pronunciation. Looking for a sound that would allow a shift, the student finds the anterior /d/. Consider that this /d/ is not the /d/ in day, but the [D] in writer or rider. The listener is choosing an allophone in English to represent a different allophone (usually considered one, but not always) in Spanish. It just happens that the allophone [D] is associated with the phoneme /d/ in L1, but it is associated with /r/, a different phoneme, in L2.

English speakers tend to interpret the intervocalic flap as a dental stop [t] or [d]. Spanish speakers assign their flap to a rhotic phoneme. This is a case where allophones in the native language are phonemes in the target language.

In conclusion, we can say that 100% of the students in this sample did perceive a different sound in this context. This can be further attested by the fact that a high number of these students chose -*v* as the spelling form, which would be the closest phonetic representation for [β] in Spanish. [β] does not exist in English. It is clearly present in Spanish, but it is not represented in Spanish orthography. We think that this *v* is used to represent [β], which would be the correct phonetic representation of this sound in Spanish. We can say that these students' perception skills are where they are supposed to be. Their production, on the other hand, is still permeated by transfer from their native language. Two students who took the test in the instructor's office pronounced out loud the form right after the instructor said it, and they produced a clear /d/ in this context. One of them asked the instructor after the test was done to pronounce the word again, which he wrote on the margin of his exam as *Teucedio*. Since the word was now pronounced in isolation, this student felt he had to somehow express the pause at the beginning, and chose a "*t*" to represent it. From these two students we had a confirmation that what they wrote was what they perceived, but no what they produced exactly. These students are still in the process of moving from L1 to L2. Parameter resetting has begun, but is not complete yet, and we should point out that it may never be complete in L2.

In their research on foreign language learning deficits, Sparks and Ganschow (1993) found a correlation between grades in the foreign language class and native language deficits. We have preliminary results that seem to indicate that this is also the case with phonemic awareness in the *Eusebio* study. Those students who chose either /b/ or /v/ had the highest scores, and those who chose /r/ had the lowest, with the ones who chose /d/ somewhere in the middle. Of course these are results for this particular test. We find that these results are right on track if we also take into account their general fluency in Spanish, observed

Phonological Processing and Second/Foreign Language Learning Difficulties 101

through informal conversations in and outside of class, and their final grade in the class.

Results from the Beginning Group

The students in the beginning group had up to three years of formal instruction in Spanish. None of them had been in a Spanish speaking country for more than a week at a time, and none of them identified themselves as having a Hispanic background. There was some initial concern about the length of study of some of the students in this group, but surprisingly there was no significant effect of this lengthy contact with the language in the results. This finding seems to be in line with the perception that for some learners, the length of contact is directly proportional to the level of acquisition, while for other learners this is not the case. This would certainly explain why more often than we would like to admit, we find students who have taken Spanish for as long as three years still enrolling in beginning courses, or not succeeding in higher level courses. There is an array of different reasons why students would chose to enroll in a lower-level class, but aside from the obvious, there is a clear perception on the part of the student about his/her possible lack of success in a higher-level class. This perception is more often than not shared by the student's advisor as well.

Table 8.6. Forms Encountered in the First-Semester Group

A.se.bi.o (1)	Us.e.dio (1)	Asebio (1)
A.den.cio (1)	a uzevéo (1)	a savío (1)
Ausavio (2)	Alocério (1)	y lu.ce.ri.o (1)
Acévio (1)	A.sill.beo (1)	No production (8)

The first thing that calls our attention about the results of this group is the consistent absence of a diphthong on the first syllable. This form was not pronounced in isolation. It came as part of the flow of speech right after the word *amigo* "friend." Pronounced within the flow of speech and coming right after an open vowel in the previous syllable, the untrained listener cannot perceive the glide –u– in this context. 33.3% of the students chose to represent what they heard with an –a–, while 33.3% were not able to write anything.

Table 8.7. *Eusebio* (masc.) (proper name)

Eu.se.bio	IO	ONSET	*CODA
a. A.se.bi.o	**	**	
b. Us.e.dio	***	*	*
c. your lu.ce.ri.o	*****	**	

In this group there was a number of students who were not able to syllabify the forms they wrote. For this reason we did not include these forms in the previous table, but we feel there are still a few things we can say about them based on what the students did, and on their comments about what they did:

Alocério: This particular instance shows a high ranking of ONSET for this learner as he introduces a consonant in between the two segments of the original diphthong. Although this learner was not able to syllabify his product, he felt the need to write and accent mark on top of what was perceived as the locus of main stress. When asked about the choice of –*a*– and –*e*– to represent *eu*– and –*e*–, this student explained he perceived a difference between the two segments.

a savío: This learner was unable to recognize this form as a proper noun and identified it as two words. The vocoid –*u*– was not represented. The learner wrote an accent mark on top of the –*i*– in order to indicate the salience of this segment. This was only one of two cases where the main stress was not identified as being on the –*e*– of the second syllable.

a uzevéo: This is a very interesting production, which at first sight looks extremely far removed from the original form. When the student was asked to pronounce what she wrote, she uttered [a.u.se.ví.o], which shows us that she was able to identify all the segments in the original form. Although she did not know how to interpret the vowels in contact in Spanish, she did hear clearly distinct vocalic segments, and chose to represent them with independent vowels. This student has not yet learned how to distinguish vocoids from vowels in Spanish, but her phonemic awareness is allowing her to identify the vocalic sounds in Spanish as different from English. She has been exposed to the notion of diacritic marks in Spanish and has chosen to write a written accent on top the vowel she perceived as stressed. It is clear that she could not identify the original stressed vowel correctly.

Differences Between the Two Groups

In the first-year group there is an even split between students who chose either *b* or *v* to represent the sound they heard, and the ones who were unable to discriminate any sound. This gives us an idea of the differences in level encountered in first year courses in most universities.

Although we have a clear improvement in the index of target productions in the advanced group: 30.7% of target b or v in the beginning group, compared with 53.8% in the advanced group, we still have 46.1% of students in the advanced group who have not completed parameter resetting for these sounds and are still associating [β] -/b/ in Spanish with [D]-[d] in English. When asked about their experience of having been exposed to the actual teaching of pronunciation, students commented that they had been quickly introduced at some point to some of the sounds in Spanish, but that this had not been practiced in detail at any point of their formal training. All of them had been given oral input in the target language, but had not been explicitly taught pronunciation. This finding raises the question of the need to teach these differences explicitly over time in the foreign language classroom. In a study done by Elliot (1997), cited by Arteaga (2000), input alone resulted in no improvement of student pronunciation, while explicit instruction yielded significant improvement. A one-semester study done with four students in a beginning Spanish class, showed improvement for only one of the four students who were explicitly taught pronunciation of voiceless stops in Spanish.[7] This represents improvement in 25% of the population. Of course, the number of participants in this study was limited, and the study will need to be replicated in order to have a better idea of the effect of explicit instruction in pronunciation.

Table 8.8. Results for [β] in First-Semester Group
(based on number of samples)

Either b and/or v	(8) 30.7%
Only b	(3) 11.5%
Only v	(5) 19.2%
Either d and/or r	(2) 7.6%
Only d	(1) 3.8%
Only r	(1) 3.8%
Only c	(1) 3.8%
No form produced	(8) 30.7%

Notes

1. Experiments with forms such as *Eusebio* work well with students at the advanced level. With non-native speakers of superior abilities it will not work because not only is their perception system now more self aware, but also there is a higher probability that they have encountered this lexical item in the written form and are now influenced by it. We can see then that even though in some cases the written form can influence production in the wrong way, in other cases it will help the speaker to identify the sounds appropriately.

2. Note that the totals do not add up to 100% because some students used more than one form.

3. We are putting together forms written with –c– and with –s– because in this context they represent the same sound, the different graphic symbol represents only an orthographic convention.

4. The –h– represents an orthographic convention and it is not pronounced in Spanish.

5. As we mentioned before –c– and –s– are orthographic conventions representing the same sound in a system where only –s– is pronounced in this environment. In a system with distinction between [θ] and [s], this type of spelling could be interpreted as violation of IO, but it is clear that in this case, the students are attempting to represent [s], and they incur in the same orthographic mistake as native speakers from a system with no distinction.

6. Again we are interpreting this spelling as a representation of [β], and therefore it does not incur in a violation of IO.

7. See Loureiro-Rodríguez, Verónica. 2001. "Las oclusivas sordas del español: problemas de asimilación en los estudiantes anglófonos. University of Colorado. Boulder, ms.

IX.
Addressing Language Learnability: How Much Information Is Enough for Learning Systems to Be Successful? Galician *geada* and Catalan *queada*

In this section we will look at how the issue of language learnability plays a role in language variation; more precisely, we will address the question of how much positive information is needed to learn a language. The examples used here come from the restructuring produced by the introduction of a new sound in Galician and Catalan in contact with Spanish, serving as a further example of changes that are produced by language contact due to speakers' perceptions of certain sounds.

Phonological phenomena, intrinsically permeated by cross-linguistic variation, like *geadas* in Galician and *queadas* in Catalan, have proven to be challenges to any theory of Universal Grammar. Directly addressing the question of language learnability (Tesar and Smolensky, 2000), Optimality Theory (Prince and Smolensky, 1993; McCarthy, 1995), with its set of universal constraints both ranked and violable, adds to the explanatory power of theories of language learning. Using a basic theory of OT, the phenomena in Galician and Catalan studied here appear to be generated by a different order in constraint ranking in Galician, Castilian Spanish, and Catalan. By explaining the Galician, Castilian, and Catalan cases, OT appears to offer a good tool not only to describe grammars in general, but also to add to the explanation of variation in languages in contact.

The first part of this section will present a brief description of the *geadas* and *queadas* and explain what they represent within the Galician and Catalan phonological systems, including a few notes of comparison between the two. The second part consists of an analysis of the *geadas* and *queadas* from an OT perspective, followed by a discussion on what contributions theories like OT offer to the learnability mechanisms involved in languages in contact.

Galician *gueadas* and *geadas*

The term "*geadas*" has been used to refer to the special pronunciation given by Western Galician speakers to /g/ and/or /x/. Although this phenomenon was first identified as a characteristic of the variety of Castilian Spanish pronounced by Galician speakers when trying to reproduce Castilian /x/, it was soon used to refer to the pronunciation of /g/ in Galician as well. Saco y Arce (1868) refers to the pronunciation of Castilian /x/ as /g/ by Galician speakers ("*gueadas*"), and Valladares Núñez (1892) uses the term "*geadas*" to refer both to the pronunciation of Castilian /x/ as /g/ and the pronunciation of Galician /g/ as /x/ ("*gueadas*" and "*geadas*"). From this point on, the term "*geadas*" was used to identify a phenomenon typical of Western Galician speech, associated with a variety of low prestige.

Spanish and Galician without *geadas*

In both Spanish and the variety of Galician without *geadas*, the phoneme /g/ is realized as: 1) a voiced velar stop [g] at the beginning of a breath group or when followed by a nasal, and 2) as a voiced velar fricative [γ] in all other environments.

Galician with *geadas*

The variety of Galician with *geadas* is characterized by the presence of what has been described as a post-velar fricative (perhaps even a faryngeal), sometimes voiced, sometimes voiceless (represented as [h] or sometimes [gh]), in all environments, except when followed by a nasal, where the voiced occlusive [g], and sometimes the voiceless [k], are found. In some speakers, [h] is realized as a voiceless velar fricative [x]. Accordingly, in the variety of Galician with *geadas*, the word *gato* "cat" can be pronounced as [gato], [hato], or [xato], and the word *domingo* "Sunday" can be pronounced as [domingo] or [dominko], or very rarely [domingho].

This phenomenon has been observed mostly in Western varieties of Galician and in isolated areas in the East. It has been attributed to Castilian influence (Pensado and Pensado Ruiz, 1983), and it has also been explained as an internal development in Galician. Here we will not go into this discussion, and we refer the reader to Pensado and Pensado Ruiz (1983) and Castro (1998) for further information on this topic.

gueadas and *queadas* in Catalan

Veny (1993) states that in Catalan, the arrival of Spanish [x] has given rise to different phenomena, among which are 1) direct import, where the Castilian form is adopted with no change: *lejía* "bleach," and 2) adaptation to a) point of articulation: *lejía=lequia*, b) manner of articulation: [le?ia].

Adaptation: /x/=/g/ *zanja=sanga*, referred to as a sporadic occurrence.

queadas: we can find *lequia* and *quicona* "Jijona" (proper name). The "*queada*," as this phenomenon is called to make a connection with Galician *geadas*, has been present in Catalonia since the eighteenth century (about the same time it was identified for Galician). This *queada* has given rise to some hypercorrection where [x] is substituted for [k]: *male[x]on* instead of *malecón* "dyke, jetty," *apo[x]inar* instead of *apoquinar* "to fork out," *o[x]aliptos* instead of *eucaliptos* "eucalyptus tree," *fin[x]a* for *finca* "property, country or rural state, farm," etc.

Veny considers Castilian /x/ as a phoneme not integrated within the Catalan system, describing it as a satellite (much in the same way as in Galician). The presence of different models of correspondence makes it possible for the same word to be adapted with different phonemes according to the different dialects or even different speakers.

Veny also mentions that processes of norm development and normalization in the language are eliminating these cases, either due to phonetic or even lexemic substitution. This parallels the situation in Galician, where the movement towards the standardization of the language is apparently contributing to the elimination of the *geada* in all but the most informal registers.

Differences and Similarities between Catalan and Galician

The previous examples help us to bring attention to the similarities and differences in both cases. The speakers of Catalan or Galician, when hearing the Castilian /x/, choose to adapt it to their systems when trying to pronounce Castilian. The obvious difference between the two systems is that in Catalan, the [x] sound has not extended to the [g] as it has in Galician. This fact is what has given rise to the idea that this phenomenon in Galician is due to the influence of the Castilian [x]. Another interesting coincidence is the fact that Catalan speakers, when hearing [x] at the beginning of the learning process, identify it with either [k] (*queadas*) or [g] (*gueadas*). Veny does not mention instances of reinterpretations like *gato*=[gh]ato in Catalan. The only examples of [x] interference in Catalan are explained as instances of hypercorrection. This hypercorrection is but one example of the problems created by this situation. Opacity is obviously a problem in the examples where [x] appears instead of [k], since it makes the original phoneme extremely difficult to identify.

Table (9.1) provides a summary of the differences and similarities in both systems.

Table 9.1. Re-Interpretation of Castilian /x/ in Galician and Catalan

Re-Interpretation	Galician	Catalan
/x/ as /k/		Quicona (for Jijona)
/x/ as /?/(sh)	xarra (for jarra)	lesia (for lejía)
/x/ as /g/	garra (for jarra)	sanga (for zanja)
/k/ as /x/		malejón (for malecón)
/g/ as /x/	[x]ato (for gato)	
/g/ as /gh/	[gh]ato (for gato)	
/g/ as /k/	dominko (for domingo)	

Guitart (1997) mentions that dialect speakers have different phonological systems comparable to second-language learners. The confusion at the beginning, that is, the *gueadas* and *queadas* both in Catalan and Galician, could be explained in this way. However, the *geadas* have existed for quite a while, and they do not seem to have the same explanation. Maybe they could have been explained that way at the beginning of the process, but not necessarily at the present time. We have to mention that *geadas* are not expected in most instances of formal speech in Galician and are only present in the fast informal register, although they are more pervasive that most scholars tend to think.[1] It should be noted that although they have been considered representative of low register and identified with poorly educated speakers, the movement towards its elimination is far from successful. The normativization of Galician has somehow slowed down the movement towards the copy of the Castilian /x/. Nevertheless, the *geadas* not associated with the /x/ or the /g/ are still present, and if the attempt of an explanation given here is on the right track, we can expect them to continue.

Tracing the evolution of these sounds, we know that in Castilian Spanish the evolution of stops from Latin to Romance followed these steps: 1) voicing of voiceless forms [p, t, k]=[b, d, g], 2) spirantization of [b, d, g] in intervocalic position, 3) sirantized forms became approximants (today in the pronunciation of these forms we barely perceive frication), and 4) deletion of spirantized forms.

Actually, this last process is still operative in Spanish, as speakers wrestle with two opposing trends: deletion or strengthening. As an example of this process we find numerous anecdotal references. We have data from a Mar de la Plata Argentinian speaker pronouncing I[gh]ual for *igual* "the same," problaby counteracting the effects of lenition by strengthening the position where the two possible pronunciations are: [iwal] with deletion or [ixual] with strengthening. Morris (2000) mentions the form di[x]usto as the result of aspiration of coda –s in the word *disgusto* "annoyance."

When Galician speakers heard this fluctuation in Castilian Spanish, they chose to strengthen it, therefore pronouncing what appeared to be [x] for the Castilian speaker. The *gueadas* are then an attempt on the part of the speaker to reproduce the approximant, while the *geadas* are an attempt to reproduce the strengthening. While Spanish today still continues to oscillate between these two tendencies, Galician appears to have chosen the second option, and it continues to do so, getting closer and closer to Castilian [x].

Bakovic (1996) proposes a fortition rule for approximants in Spanish, following Lozano's (1979) idea that Cuban Spanish has the fricatives, and not the stops, as the underlying form. It is possible that Galician had the fricatives as the deep structure as well when Castilian [x] was introduced, and this situation allowed the speakers to choose the fricative variant to reproduce it. Processes like this, triggered by languages in contact, indicate the role played by the listener in the initiation of sound change, as discussed by Holt (1997). We can study this phenomenon from different points of view, and we refer the reader to Pensado and Pensado Ruiz (1983) and Castro (1998), among others, for more detailed discussions.

OT Analysis of *geadas* and *queadas*

In this section we will look at the outputs given by the *geada* from the point of view of OT to see if this theory helps in clarifying the processes at hand. Since the basic concepts of OT have already been introduced in previous chapters, in this section we will only review those ideas pertinent to the issue at hand.

McCarthy (1995) has advanced OT by incorporating what it is now called Correspondence Theory. According to this theory, there is a group of constraints called "Faithfulness constraints," which are:

1. MAX: the surface form should maximally retain underlying features or segments (it substitutes PARSE in the Prince and Smolensky framework). This constraint says that no feature or segment should be deleted.

2. IDENT(ity)-[F]: input and output segments have the same values for a particular feature, place, etc.

3. DEP(endency) (FILL in Prince and Smolensky's framework): output forms should depend on underlying forms. This constraint prevents insertion or epenthesis.

We will also use two constraints posited by Bakovic (1996):

1. STRONG ONSET: he uses this constraint to insert an oral closure breath-group-initially before underlying approximants to create stops. Here it will be used for the same purpose; however, it will not be applied to an approximant as the underlying structure but to a neutralized G that will be realized as a stop when following a sound with that characteristic.

2. CONTIGUITY: an input representation must be parsed into a contiguous non-interrupted string. This will explain the re-syllabification processes in languages like Spanish in which syllables tend to link to each other in specific environments.

And we will introduce our own two constraints:

1. *STRONG CODA: disallows the presence of stops in syllable and word final position.

2. *STRONG INTERVOC: disallows the presence of voiced stops in inter-vocalic position.

These constraints are summarized in Table 9.2.

Table 9.2. Summary of OT Constraints

McCarthy (1995), Faithfulness constraints	1. MAX(imization): no feature or segment should be deleted (PARSE in Prince and Smolensky framework). 2. IDENT(ity): input and output segments have the same values for a particular feature, place, etc. 3. DEP(endency): no insertion or epenthesis (FILL in Prince and Smolensky framework).
Bakovic (1996)	4. STRONG ONSET: inserts an oral closure breath-group-initially. 5. CONTIGUITY: an input representation must be parsed into a contiguous non-interrupted string.
Added in the present study	6. *STRONG CODA: no stops in syllable and word final position. 7. *STRONG INTERVOC: no voiced stops in between vowels.

Data Analysis

In Spanish, nasals must have the same place of articulation as the following obstruent: homorganic clusters must agree in place. Nasals also pass on their oral closure to the obstruent, causing the obstruent to surface as an occlusive if we postulate the fricative as the underlying form in Spanish. If we posit the stop as the underlying form, we need to have a way to explain the fricative variants. But if we consider the concept of neutralization in certain positions and go back to the concept of the Archiphoneme, we may help explain these problems. If what we have is a neutral G that is only defined as a velar—that is, the only important features are those for point of articulation (place)—then the speaker can choose to have as a phonetic manifestation any of the sounds in question. This would be true for Galician at least, but not necessarily for Spanish. One thing that comes to mind is the tendency of /b, d, g/ in Spanish to be pronounced as stops, even in environments where the fricative or approximant would be expected. This tends to occur in situations where Spanish is in contact with other native languages. We can see that at first, one of the pronunciations of /g/ in Galician, as well as Catalan, was precisely the stop, not /g/ but /k/, as manifested in the *queadas*.

Table 9.3. Castilian System

/Gato/	STRONG ONSET	IDENT
☞ a. gato		
b. yato	*!	*!
c. kato		*!

In Table 9.3, the occlusive [g] emerges as the winner in (a). It is the norm in Castilian Spanish that after a pause and in absolute initial position, we encounter the occlusive variant [g]. In this environment STRONG ONSET is the highest-ranked constraint. CONTIGUITY does not play a role, as the word is pronounced in isolation. This state of events changes within the context of discourse. At this point, the ranking between IDENT and STRONG ONSET is not clear, although we could think that IDENT is the highest-ranked, since it only takes a violation of IDENT to eliminate [kato] as the winning candidate. We will see later that it would not be wise to rank these two constraints at this point.

Table 9.4. Castilian System (within a phrase)

/el Gato/	CONTIGUITY	IDENT	STRONG ONSET
a. el gato	*!		
☞b. el γato		*!	*!
c. el kato	*!	*!	

When the word *gato* is inserted within a phrase, we can see that STRONG ONSET is no longer the highest-ranked constraint. As mentioned before, we could try to say that IDENT is the highest-ranked constraint in Table 9.3, but if we do so, we would not be able to explain why it is demoted in Table 9.4, where CONTIGUITY emerges as the highest-ranked. Observe that although (b) in 9.4 violates two constraints, it still emerges as the winning output in this environment because it does not violate the higher-ranked CONTIGUITY.

In Table 9.5 we see what happens when the sound in question is preceded by a nasal stop. In this case STRONG ONSET becomes the higher-ranked constraint.

Table 9.5. Castilian System (preceded by a nasal)

/DomiNGo/	STRONG ONSET	*STRONG CODA	IDENT
a. domingo		*!	
b. domiɲγo	*!		*!*!
☞c. domiŋgo			*!
d. domiŋko			*!*!

Observe that the only constraint that differentiates between (c), the winning candidate, and (d) is one extra violation of IDENTITY in (d).

Table 9.6. Galician System with *geadas*

/Gato/	CONTIGUITY	STRONG ONSET	IDENT
a. gato	*!		
☞b. ghato		*!	*!
c. kato	*!		*!

Notice that in Table 9.6 CONTIGUITY should not play a role since the word is pronounced in isolation, but since Galician seems to favor the fricative variant, even in initial position, we will use this constraint to signal this fact. (b) violates both STRONG ONSET and IDENT. Remember that the input we are postulating for the *geadas* is not /g/, but a neutralized /G/. (c) violates only CONTIGUITY and IDENT, and it seems to be marked, even within the *geadas* system, as low prestige. In the Galician system that favors *geadas*, we find that (b) emerges as the winning candidate.

Table 9.7. Galician System with *geadas* (within a phrase)

/o Gato/	CONTIGUITY	STRONG ONSET	IDENT
a. o gato	*!	*!	
☞b. o ghato		*	*
c. o kato	*!		*!

Note that (b) in Table 9.7 wins for the same reasons that (b) wins for Spanish in Table 9.4, but the actual realization of this sound is different in both languages.

Table 9.8. Galician System with *geadas* (preceded by a nasal sound)

/domiNGo/	STRONG ONSET	*STRONG CODA	CONTIGUITY	IDENT
a. domingo		*!	*	
b. domiɲyo	*!			*
☞c. domiŋgo			*	
☞d. domiŋko			*	*
☞e. domiŋxo	*!			*

In Table 9.8, candidates (c) and (d) win if STRONG ONSET is the highest ranked constraint, but if CONTIGUITY is ranked higher, (e) is the winner. We find examples of all these three instances within the geada system.

Table 9.9. Galician without *geada*

/domiNGo/	STRONG ONSET	*STRONG CODA	VOICE	MAX	ID PL
a. domingo		*!		*	*
b. domiɲyo	*!			**	**
☞c. domiŋgo				*	**
e. domiŋko			*!	**	**

In Table 9.9, (c) is the winner, and (e) is next in terms of feasibility. This is exactly what happens in the Galician system with *geada*.

In Galician, for the dialect that produces "dominko," the constraint with the highest rank is ID PL; therefore, the output has to be the occlusive, and the only possible one available is voiceless. For the dialect that produces "domingho," the higher-ranked constraint is CONTIGUITY.

Addressing Language Learnability

Table 9.10. A Look at *gueadas* within Galician

/aGuGa/	Contiguity	ID PL	Voice	Strong Onset
a. aguxa	*!	*	* (?)	*
☞b. aghugha			* (?)	*!*!
c. aguga	*!*!			*!*!
☞d. axuxa			*! (?)	
e. axuga	*!	*!		

Observe that in Table 9.10 we identify two possible winners. Both of these forms are attested with the *geadas*. What is relevant is the fact that Contiguity is ranked higher than Strong Onset and therefore marks the winners. There is a question mark following Voice because in Galician we find instances of both voiceless and voiced manifestations of these forms. Voice is introduced in the table solely for illustrative purposes.

The Catalan System

In the Catalan system we have no examples of the movement of /g/ to /h/ or /gh/. The instances that have been reported show one of three possibilities of re-presentation: 1) the use of one sound already present in the language: *lejia–lesia*, 2) the adoption of the foreign sound without re-interpretation: *lejia*, and 3) the adaptation of the foreign sound to the closest sound in the language: *lejia–lequía*. In Table 9.11, it seems that the operative feature value is [Ident Voice]. Since the sound the Catalan speaker hears is voiceless [x], the closest adaptation would be the voiceless velar [k]. Observe that the identification [x]=[g] is very sporadic. It has only been observed in examples like *zanja–sanga*, where there is a nasal present that requires the formation of a homorganic cluster. Strong Onset seems to be highly ranked in Catalan as well, and we can see it at work in cases explained through hypercorrection. These cases are probably the result of the interaction between both the Voice and Strong Onset constraints.

Table 9.11. The Catalan System

/lexía/	Strong Onset	Ident Voice	*Strong Interv
☞a. lekía			*
b. lexía	*!		
d. leγía	*!	*!	

Conclusions and Questions

It appears that in Spanish the higher-ranked constraint is STRONG ONSET, making the initial position after a pause and after nasals the deciding factors for the appearance of the stop, while other positions are open to the fricative or approximant. In this situation, the speaker can oscillate between conflicting systems: 1) fortition (to avoid violating MAX) or 2) lenition which can (and does) produce deletion (violating MAX, but satisfying *STRONG CODA).

We still need to look at these processes in more detail. They may be two different constraints. There is even the possibility that they are two conflicting constraints, because one is weakening or deleting consonants in coda position to maintain the CV pattern, while the other is deleting a consonant in inter-vocalic position, breaking the CV pattern. What is interesting is that both processes involve consonant weakening of some sort within a word or in the discourse, therefore favoring CONTIGUITY as the higher-ranked constraint.

In Catalan, the operative constraints seem to be STRONG ONSET and IDENT VOICE, while in the system with geadas in Galician, CONTIGUITY seems to be the top ranked constraint.

These differences in constraint rankings have important implications for language learning. In Galician, the fricative seems to have been the underlying form. When Castilian /x/ and /g/ came into the picture, oscillating between lenition and/or strengthening, Galician speakers did not have enough overt examples of these two sounds to assess the distinction completely. Due to this lack of positive information, the learned system allows for fluctuation even today. For the native Spanish speaker, the presence of /x/ as a distinctive phoneme restricts the fluctuation and does not allow [g] to go all the way to /x/, although we do hear a sound close to /x/ in some native Spanish speakers when they attempt to pronounce /g/. In Catalan, the hypercorrection cases could be explained the same way. The small number of cases present does not provide enough input to facilitate complete control of the distinction.

We have seen that the cases studied in this chapter present a great degree of variation, but even within such varied systems there are certain constraints that, by being highly ranked, favor certain occurrences and not others. In Galician, CONTIGUITY is ranked higher than STRONG ONSET, and therefore, in the *geada* varieties, [o ghato] wins over [o gato]. Notice that [o ghato] also wins over [o γato] because this last one violates [MAX].

Notes

1. Since Galician was not considered to be the language of culture for a long time, it is only natural that phenomena specific to Galician were only used in informal situations and therefore associated with low prestige.

Appendix I.
Data Taken from López Fornat (1994)

Age	Track	Child Form	Target Form
1:07	001	gue	qué
		tene	tiene
	008	má	más
	009	aúpa	
		pé	pie
	010	má	mano
	011	notá	no está
		aguá	agua
		ete	este
	014	amí	a dormir
	019	a mir	a dormir
		no'sta	no están
		aio	adiós
	020	maa	mamá
		má	mala
		pa e má	papá es malo
	024	eta	esta
	025	ven	ven
	027	Quimeno	
		Capena	
		ista	esta
		istche	chiste[1]
	028	pí	lápiz
		asia	gracias
	029	amiamo	llamamos
		gasia	gracias
	030	guauguau	
	031	zapá	zapato

032	a pí	a pintar
	ñeque	?
033	mañá	mañana
034	aios	adiós
035	queque	muñeco
	Acaña	Encarna
036	Anti	Santi (Santiago?)
037	nos'tá	no está
	Bis	Luis
038	maia	mala
	má	malo
039	tas, tas	pegar
		(onomatopoeic form)
042	aió	adiós
043	éste	éste
	mamá, éste[2]	mamá, ésta
	papá, éste	papá, éste
044	men	ven
045	abaa	agua
	apiíta	tapita
	apá	tapa, tapar
047	acá a má	a secar la mano
048	asias	gracias
050	acar/acá	secar
051	poquí	por qué
	po qué[3]	por qué
	paquí	por qué
	pooquée (yelling)	por qué
052	os'tá e miau	dónde está el gato
053	tes	tres
055	pés	pies
	ete	este
057	o'stá	dónde está
	ostá	dónde está
058	nos'tá	no está
059	mía	mira
	ía	mira
060	oe	coche
	cote	coche
062	ati	Santi
	ombe	hombre
067	oe	colores
	amadillo	amarillo
	veye	verde
	tita	blanquita

Apendix I

	069	apá	papá
		etita	tetita
	070	apá	a tapar
		apa	tapa
1:08	072	n'otá má	no está mamá
	074	quitín	chiquitín
		aande	grande
		aquí, tá	aquí está
	075	tó	tos
	077	osé	no sé
	079	soso	el oso/los osos[4]
	080	Cana	Encarna
		notá	no está
		ostá	no está
	081	ostá	dónde está
	082	buá	guardar
	083	apatos	zapatos
	085	poco	tampoco
	086	acá[5]	caer/se ha caído
	087	este silla	esta silla
	088	ete oto	este otro
		ota	otra
		cachá	cacharro
	089	ee aquí	vete de aquí
	090	tás	sientas/siéntate?
	092	toto	tonto
		collá	collar
	094	buaubuá	perro
		buaubá	
		guauguau	
1:09	101	suto/susto	susto
	102	íto	quito
	103	o tá	dónde está
	104	abua	agua
	106	tasto	trasto
		mé/mee	bien
		má	mal
	107	otá	dónde está
	109	aba	agua
	111	ti(s)ta/tista	triste
	113	ya'stá/ya etá	ya está
	114	lus	luz
	123	a tisú/achús	
	123	ya está	
		tonto	

128		meia/éte maia	media(s)/estas medias
132		lolot	dodot
134		roto	
		aió	adiós
		bollo/collo	rollo
		tista/tita triste	
		loto	roto
137		apatos/epatos	zapatos
		niz	nariz
		ocho	ojos
		tá	cara
		cabesa	cabeza
138		mañana	
		cachis/casis	mecachis
		suso	susto
139		callá	cállate
140		opita	solita
143		salta	
		ota	otra
		coto	coche
145		malo	
146		sento/siento	siento
		sienta	siéntate
147		pa-yá	para allá
148		llueve	
150		listo	
		achó	la flor
153		ete	este
		chó	flor
		Maía	María
154		toos	todos
155		pincha	
		cachis	mecachis
156		saltá	saltar
158		patatas	
162		bota/buta	(re)bota
163		ía	mira
		ya estáa ya está	
164		eto	esto
		cahaqueta/chaqueta	
		azú	azul
165		pie	
166		ete/ésta	éste/ésta
		flol	flor
		pita	pincha

Apendix I

		cota	corta
	168	ota	otra
		siento	
		benas	buenas
	169	coshes	coches
1:10	170	sicó/osicó	un chico
	171	sico	triciclo
	173	llaleta	galleta
	174	oto pe	otro pie
		sito/sienta	
	176	María	
		Teo/Teíto	
		Maniam Marian	
	178	toló	dodot
	179	balletas servilletas	
	180	buá	guardar
	181	oto pato otro plato	
	182	cogé	coger
		butota	botella
	183	potito	poquito
		yo	
	185	mía	mira
	186	llove	llueve
		abochá	abrochar
	187	medisina	medicina
		la tos	
	188	azúu, asú azul	
		ota	otra
		felíi	feliz
		vola	vuela
	189	s'a acabao	se ha acabado
	191	pate	parte
		usana	Susana
	192	maio	mayo
		alitas/alito/	
		palito	palomitas
	193	parez	pared
	194	pa(r)tí/	partir
		yatá patí	ya está partido
	195	paré	pared
		asú	azul
		banca	blanca
		paiés/parés	pared
		teshe, tesho	techo
	196	Pilá	Pilar

Appendix I

197	máncas	mangas
	sou-bá	a subir
198	vée	ven
	Mañián	Marian
	Yastá	ya está
202	mámoo	vamos
203	vosotos	vosotros
	nosotos	nosotros
204	soñá	soñar
	vamo	vamos
	a tudiá/astudiá/estudiá/	a estudiar
	vena	venga
205	siquinina	chiquitina
	coento	cuento
	pintá	pintar
	lápis	lapiz
	pila	peli/película
206	aia	hala
	ábelo	ábrelo
208	mámo	vamos
209	libo	libro
	sapatitos	zapatitos
210	velas/velás	verás
	mano/manó	mano
	yito	payasito
	só	sol
211	saqueta	chaqueta
	botó/bonto	botón
212	(m)otá	montar/montas
	se cá	se cae
	Manina María	
	Tedito	Teíto
	Mañián Marián	
217	tidito	Teíto
	papo	guapo
	papa	guapa
	tamén	también
218	naie	nadie
219	bavoo	bravo
	ía	mira
220	reló	reloj
221	pué	puré
	po(s)te	postre
	masana	manzana
222	Manía	María

Apendix I

	224	pachito	pasito
	226	evanta	levántame
		po(r)sa	por favor
		sacabó	se acabó
	228	Cáa	Ricardo
		Anina	Anita
		Os	los
		Piláa	Pilar
	232	cái	cae
		tipitito	chiquitito
	233	madito	malito
	234	judo	junio
	235	An(k/gees)	Ángeles
		Aankees Ángeles	
		Angée	Ángeles
		Manía	María
	237	M'a chupao	me ha chupado
		coshino cochino	
	238	S'a pedido/perdido	se ha perdido
		fato	falta
		a vé	a ver
		s'a loto	se ha roto
	239	póme	ponme
	-240	cajaguillo	gargajillo
	241	isico	triciclo
		Mabée	Mabel
	243	Calitos	Carlitos
		dálee	darle
		peñas	piernas
	245	sintá	cinta
		sapato	zapato
		vedito	vestidito
		didito/dedito	dedito
		uñas	
		añís	nariz
		pondiente	pendiente
		agosita	orejita
		pilitos	pelitos
		basito	bracito
		peñaa	pierna
		tipita	tripita
		Píeee	pie
1:11	246	casines	calcetines
	247	mi cái	me caigo

Appendix I

248	e mí	es mío
	pantón	pantalón
249	parée	pared
250	parées	pared
	asúu	azul
	blanco	
	pantó	pantalón
	amísa	camisa
	botón	
	oto botóon	otro botón
	ota botona	otra botona
	collá	collar
	más	
251	satalillo	se ha caido
	sacalillo	se ha caido
253	escusha	escucha
	a calláa	a callar
255	(D)éjale/éjale	déjale
	sentá	sentar
256	supa	chupa
	cusara	cuchara
257	entá	sentar
	abe	abre
258	jobetes	juguetes
	mu	muy
	kamón	jamón
259	galleta	
260	maminita	maquinita
261	s'a pirao	se ha pillado
262	suso	sucio
	pie	
	tene	tiene
	poque	porque
263	calso tée/cáso	cálzate
	ombée	hombre
	ponco	pongo
	semponga	se ponga
	tamén	también
264	camelito	caramelito
	fefa	fresa
	sicolota	chocolate
	pistasho	pistacho
	tapoco	tampoco
266	cáin	caen
	avantado	levantado

Apendix I

		goro	gorro
		copota	capota
	267	domida	dormida
		esquibí	escribir
		teno	tengo
	268	caló	calor
	271	mojcas	moscas
	272	peda/piedas	piedra/piedras
	275	cotita/cutita	gotita
	276	señoíta	señorita
	277	peiá	peinar
	278	cumpeaños	cumpleaños
		felis	feliz
2:00	279	gansas	naranjas
		pitinos	plátanos
	280	sabu/s'a buscao	se ha buscado
		bañano	bañarnos
		coche	
	281	manzanas	
		tamén	también
		sopá	soplar
		táltaa	tarta
	282	pernas	piernas
	283	Lui	Luis
		talta	tarta
	284	sobla	sopla
		bié	bien
		yatá	ya está
		ya está	
		ota ve(z)	otra vez
	285	s'a muscao	se ha chamuscado
		seá	será
	287	vé	ver
		a mí	a dormir
		loso	los ojos
		cena	cierra
		lositos	los ojitos
		quero	quiero
		shusta	gusta
	290	talta	
		ta(l/r)ta	tarta
		bieón	biberón
	291	piquinita/pequenita	pequeñita
	293	mojca	mosca
		as moscas	las moscas

		feiyas	feas
		posas	mariposas
	299	sí tá	está
		tá bucando	está buscando
	303	hipo-cóntano	hipopótamo
		se ñama	se llama
	305	Galisia	Galicia
		co	con
		notá	no está
	306	Ima	Irma
	308	golito	gorgorito
		gorito	gorgorito
		Maniña	Marina
	309	se paga	se apaga
	312	conto	cuento (noun)
	313	oiendo	poniendo
		quero	quiero
	314	pomnes	pones
		tae	trae
		po favó	por favor
		gasias	gracias
	315	ío	tío
		ota ves	otra vez
	316	gompe	rompe
		guompe	rompe
	317	cumparanta	cumpleaños
		hase caló	hace calor
	318	enconse	entonces
		tabajá	trabajar
		pobesita	pobrecita
		quere	quiere
		s'a caído	se ha caído
		s'a deishao	se ha duchado
		co jabón	con jabón
		s'aillo	se ha ido
		mía	mira
		escuses	escucha
		estesun	este es un
		oto	otro
	319	jabo	jabón
		no'stán	no está
		pisina	piscina
		pitina	piscina
		jubando	jugando
2:01	320	terrasa	terraza

Apendix I

321	pa montá	para montar
	cumpeaños/cumpeanos/cumparata	
		cumpleaños
	feliz	
322	Galisia	Galicia
	sapatilla	zapatilla
	conejitos	
	para	parra
	notá conegito	no está el conejito
323	cáo	claro
	mosiña	mociña
324	asú	azul
326	págalo	apágalo
	poque	porque
	pos que	por que
328	taba	estaba
	madita	malita
	Cafita gosa	Caperucita Roja
	Tonses	entonces
	Capusita	Caperucita
	Ota cosa má	otra cosa más
	Conto	cuento
329	bailá	bailar
	sivillanas	Sevillanas
	e vestido	el vestido
331	m'a compao	me ha comprado
	uno sapato	unos zapatos
	tene	tiene
	mushos	muchos
	mentiosa	mentirosa
332	abe la pielta	abre la puerta
	po favó	por favor
	aquerosa	asquerosa
	pedó	perdón
333	tes sardina	tres sardinas
	pala limpiá	para limpiar
334	o milo	lo miro
	ziñó/señó	señor
	tero	quiero
335	eso zapato(s)	esos zapatos
	bu(s)cá	buscar
	c(l)ase	clase
336	pared	
337	ayiba	arriba

Appendix I

	a(s)	las
338	quié	quiere
	queres	quieres
340	amos a…cantá	vamos a cantar
	Maena	Manea?
	Tae la ma	trae la mano?
	Ota vé	otra vez
	Disce	dice
	Calitos	Carlitos
341	hambé	hambre
342	cane	carne
343	palaguas	paraguas
	glande	grande
	quiero/quero	
344	cacharito	cacharrito
	terrasa	terraza
	ponlohí	ponlo ahí
345	te ha taído	te ha traído
	(l)evanto	levanto
	riba	arriba
346	tabajando	trabajando
	ganito	granito
	tie mucha() cosá que hasé	
	tiene muchas cosas que hacer	
347	se me cague e gorro	se me cae el gorro
349	poro	puedo
	abando	hablando
350	una bocata	un bocata
	shoriso	chorizo
	podo/puede	
351	ginapsia	gimnasia
352	agantá	arrancar
353	Do…tea	Dorotea
354	ompiendo	rompiendo
356	pedone	perdone
357	trabajando	
	arrancar	
358	sétate	siéntate
	popo	pongo
361	tieno	tengo
362	te volamatá	te voy a matar
	hómee	hombre
363	femini/fememinina	femenina
365	piluletas/puruletas	piruletas

Apendix I

	367	Agée/Ageles	Ángeles
		ste	siete
	368	camelos	caramelos
		oto s'a salío/sailo/	salido
			otro se ha salido
		suso	sucio
		abemelo	ábremelo
	369	sangüis	sandwich
	370	popote	hipopótamo
	371	Mía yo tamén quero hasé una peli	Mira yo también quiero hacer una peli
		Contillao	contigo yo/ahora?
	372	negos	negros
2:02	374	sanguish	sandwich
	376	guzta/gusta	gusta
	380	dusha	ducha
		jubáar/jugbáar	jugar
		juguetes	
		pe(s)cao	pescado
		pe(z)te	pestes
	381	todos/todod	
	382	ere mu guapo	eres muy guapo
		guadalo/guádalos	guárdalos
		guardarlos	
		Isioro	Isidoro
	384	tambié	también
		co papá	con...
		al paque	al parque
	385	mi melto	me he muerto
		aganta	garganta
	386	eta pa mi	esta para mí
		hovos	huevos
		sachichas	salchichas
		fruta	
	387	serra	cierra
		pernas	piernas
		volvo	vuelvo
	389	juebo	juego
		jubando	jugando
		puente	
	390	bolo	lobo[6]
	392	me ágo	me ahogo
		co/con u camelo	con un caramelo
		a sustado	ha/he asustado?
	394	va po el teléfono	va a por el

Appendix I

			teléfono
		futa	fruta
		surros de'sos	churros de esos
	395	te vo	te voy
	396	buenísima	
	399	busta	gusta
	401	me duele un ojo	
	402	teno que lavá este cacharo	tengo que lavar este cacharro
		tieno siebe	tengo fiebre
	406	miña mi guapa	niña muy guapa
		uja/buja piruja	bruja piruja
		tesusto	te asusto
	407	Banca Nieves	Blanca Nieves
	408	efiá	enfriar
		muso fío	mucho frío
		los leotardo/lotardos/lotaldos	leotardos
	409	timbe	timbre
		tipita	tripita
		bigo/ombigo	ombligo
		tá pequeño	está pequeño
		o(r)a	ahora
		leotaldos	leotardos
		mira/miámelos	mira/míramelos
	410	gualdas	largas
	411	pombo	pongo
		abóchame	abróchame
		palitos	zapatitos
2:03	413	pompa	ponga? Poner? Pone?
	414	etoy	estoy
	415	pómpala	ponla?
		Pompo	pongo
		No mascuches	no me escuches
		Hombe	hombre
	416	círculo	
	417	tabajá	trabajar
		home	hombre
	420	fegao las pantitas	regado las plantitas
		regá	regar
		pegá las pantitas	regar las plantitas
	421	un choche	un coche
		oto coche	otro coche
		pa abí la perta	para abrir la

			puerta
	422	pompar	poner
		jugá	jugaba?
		Etaba…jugá	estaba jugando?
		Jubando	jugando
		Bolo feroz	lobo feroz
	425	Victor	
		Taé	traer
	427	Pulgacito	Pulgarcito
	428	liblo	libro
		voy a leélo	voy a leerlo
	429	parque	
		colelos	colores
	434	pipótamo	hipopótamo
	437	corasant	croissant
	438	pulper	puzzle
	439	purle	puzzle
	441	trago gande	trago grande
		mu gandes	muy grandes
		pimero	primero
	442	Jalicia	Galicia
		güelo	luego
2:04	445	encuento	encuentro
	448	hipopótamo/hipopót/hipopó	
	449	pipótamo	hipopótamo
	450	amarilla,roja,verde	
		pueltas	puertas
	451	un castillo	
		mu gande	muy grande
		oto	otro
	453	negas	negras
	454	sopando	soplando
		poque	porque
	455	juba	jugar
		contillo	contigo
		ara	ahora
		spero	espero
	456	fesa	fresa
	457	devolvido	devuelto
	458	tá e su suna	esta es su cuna
		agós	arroz
		yojo	y ojo
	459	po/poque	porque
		fío	frío
2:05	460	el bolo, el lobo feroz	

Appendix I

	460	sodorante	desodorante
		giendo	riendo
		sacarme	
	462	toballa	toalla
		pómpamelo	pónmelo
	466	pompo	pongo
		nobes	nombres
		Mániam	Marian
	467	pompá	poner
		pongo	
	468	Pepito,Pedito	Pedrito
	471	poméme	ponerme
	472	conmío	conmigo
	473	bosque/bojque	
		lobo/bolo	
		peinar/peiná	
	475	eto també	esto también
	482	fío/frío	
	484	poqué	por qué
		quemita	cremita
	487	la meisinas	las medicinas
		dormir	
		tabajá	trabajar
	488	otas	otras
	489	po qué	por qué
		quero	quiero
		tanvía	tranvía
		gande	grande
		logo	luego
	490	corilos/cocodilo	cocodrilo/s
	492	siego	cierro
		segar	cerrar
		segado	cerrado
		toballas	toallas
	493	(s)tán	están
		abugujadas	arrugadas
		aguban	arrugan
	494	ponto	pronto
		oto	otro
2:06	496	peña	pierna
	497	liblo	libro
	498	mu	muy
	500	peguito	perrito
		tes y cuato	tres y cuatro
		pego	perro

Apendix I

	501	gande	grande
		tontuga	tonturria
	503	jugar/jubar	
	504	azul	
		cuadado	cuadrado
		cículo	círculo
		cuaditos	cuadraditos
		juebes	juegues
		cegag	cerrar
	506	pistina	piscina
	509	puertecita	
2:07	510	jersey	
	515	eto	esto
		oto	otro
	519	estás gordísima	
	522	tipa	tripa
	524	molinillo	
		fútbol/furbol	
		abíle/abílo	abrirle/lo
	525	escugo	escurro
2:08	526	vemtiseis	veintiseis
		pistina	piscina
		tegasa	terraza
	528	gande	grande
		cafetito	cafecito
		otro	
		gojo	rojo
		pego	perro
		jubete	juguete
		cachaguito	cacharrito
	531	azuquítar	
		garganta	
	533	gandísima	grandísima
		cái	cae
	539	Almudena	
	540	Apongo/apoyo	apoyo
		Escugo	escurro
2:09	541	cuatro de abril del ochenta y nueve	
		tozo	trozo
		pompó	puso
		mu	muy
		goda	gorra
	544	lobo	
		gorito	gorrito
		aguiba	arriba

		venieron	vinieron
		abieron	abrieron
		gandes	grandes
		grande	
		tipa	tripa
	548	cierra	
		peñas	piernas
		cárcel	
	550	psicólaga	psicóloga
	551	jugando/jubando	
		gandes	grandes
	552	pómpate	ponte
	553	biciqueta	bicicleta
		alpiste	
	555	geloj	reloj
		el otro ojo	
2:11	558	María	
	559	Marde/madre	
	560		Paya
		playa	
			Cachaguito
		cacharrito	
			Gosa
		rosa	
			Tenerlo
	562	sequeto	secreto
		tes y cuato	tres y cuatro
		comparme una tarta	comprarme una tarta
		cómalas, cómelas comerlas?	
		Compes	compres
		Soparlas	soplarlas
		Siesta	fiesta
		Bancanieves	Blanca…
		Madasta	madrastra
		Ente	entre (entrar)
		Caro	claro
	563	velo/verlo	verlo
		taído	traído
		peine	
		peno	peino
		peinar	
	564	ponerme	
		ponémelas	ponermelas
	565	caro	claro

Apendix I   133

	566	tipa	tripa
		trabajo/tabajo	trabajo
		gápida	rápida
		Bancanieves	Blanca…
		Goja	roja
		Tralaralarito	
		Abuelita	
		Bojque	bosque
		Gande	grande
		Babacito	garbancito?
			Pulgarcito?
		Compar	comprar
		Hombe	hombre
	567	pego	perro
		ota	otra
		médico	
		guelo	luego
	568	vajca	vasca
3:01	570	gora	gorra
		voltereta	
		merienda	
	576	collo	cuello
		playa	
	577	galar	guardar
	578	la buja	la bruja
		abujero	agujero
		ten	tren
		atás	atrás
	579	tocito	trocito
	580	en inglés	
		piedas	piedras
	581	ota	otra
	582	Mardid	Madrid
	583	Madid	Madrid
3:06	584	tres	
		tabajao	trabajado
		concencionistas	concepcionistas
	585	siempe/simpe	siempre
	586	esamen	examen
		liblo	libro
		b/guena	
	587	pueta	puerta
	588	blazo	brazo
		luego	
	590	bolígrafo	

	591	bibirón	biberón
3:07	594	la mosca	
	597	claro	
	601	los ties	los tres
	602	los prismáticos	
	604	biazos	brazos
		máquina	
	608	ties moscas	tres moscas
	609	mentirijillas	
	610	cuato	cuatro
	613	peo	pero
	617	he estopeao	estropeado
	622	granja/granjero	
		colo	cuelo (colar)
		caballero (caballo)	
		pescadero (pescados)	
		libradero (libros) librero	
		monero (monos)	
		frutero (frutas)	
		carnero (carne)	
		pesetero (pesetas)	
		ventanero (ventanas)	
		vaquero-vacas	
		tendero (tiendas)	
		gorrero (gorras)	
		pelero (pelo)	
3:09	624	ijquierdo	
		blandito	
	634	olelá	olerla
		postie/poste	postre
	635	mientas	mientras
		fío	frío
	638	busiluz	Gusiluz
3:10	644	perifagilísticoespialidoso	
	645	las cinco y cuarto	
	648	házsela	

Notes

1. Considering the complexity of this form at such an early age, we cannot be sure if this is the child's form for *chiste* "joke" or another form for *este* "this," which is emphasized in the dialogue.

2. The mother corrects the girl and says *mamá, ésta*.

3. The mother says the target form several times, which produces different forms from the girl.

4. The mother asks for *los osos* and the girl says *soso* y luego *ososo*. [s] seems to be associated with the ONSET.

5. In the data *acá* is listed as *caer*, but it looks like a truncated form of *se ha caido*.

6. It is the father who starts saying *bolo*, and the girl goes along with it. It is interesting, though, that in this track the father insists on saying *Tacirupeca*, which is *Caperucita* backwards, but the girl does not repeat it until the very end, when she says the same exact form—*Tacirupeca*—twice. The father utters *Cacirupeca* once and *Tacirupeca* six times.

Appendix II.
Examples of Grammatical Gender Transfer

I. Feminine in Spanish–Masculine in English
1. el password (si lo cambié)–La clave, la contraseña
2. del Playboy (la revista Playboy)
3. el cockpit, cockpit voice recorder–La cabina (la grabadora/el grabador)
4. hacer un set up (una instalación)
5. porque no esto no es, no es profit no es si no que es un servicio
6. un Ovation cuerda de nailon
7. el shower
8. el shopping
9. el Master (la maestría, pero en España "el master")
10. un day care (la guardería)
11. el freeway
12. el headquarters (la sede, la oficina central, pero también el cuartel general)
13. un bypass (una anastomosis) (operación)
14. esos tickets (entradas, pero también billetes)
15. un computer science (especialidad, carrera)
16. los muebles del living (la sala)
17. el FDA (la oficina, la administración)
18. a un open house
19. el Play-Do (la plastilina)

II. Masculine in Spanish–Masculine in English

1. del MetLine íbamos a tomar otro que es más amplio
2. en el downtown Chicago
3. un mínimo de usage
4. el abstract
5. unos Levy's
6. un bill of lading?
7. al daddy
8. el brown (el color)
9. el blue jean
10. los malls
11. son business si no los abres
12. tipo del news and Observe (periódico)
13. del rally (periódico)
14. como fan brasileño
15. el mail
16. un standard
17. la oficina del lease (arrendamiento, alquiler)
18. el leasing
19. del college (tomado como colegio, no como universidad)
20. al country
21. del PIN
22. el CD
23. el casete
24. el station (el carro)
25. los pampers
26. el Citi Bank
27. el mouth piece (el auricular)
28. los sandwiches
29. los US hostels
30. un day care (el hogar de cuidado diario, el nido)
31. el Medical College
32. el lunch
33. al counter
34. al health food (restaurante?, Mercado?)
35. este software (el programa)
36. un freezer (congelador, pero también heladera)
37. esos tickets (billetes, pero también entradas)
38. el spring (el muelle, el resorte)
39. el Michael's (refers to the store: tienda/almacén, the same as in el Corte Inglés)
40. los muebles del living (el salón)
41. el flash
42. el FDA (el ministerio, el departamento)

43. del rock (el rock and roll)
44. el que era mi roommate
45. a hacer el strip?
46. el Pacific
47. un ring
48. el show
49. al nine one, one—
50. ese service
51. después del Labor Day
52. es un, St. Mary's College, uno católico
53. los rolling stones
54. un roommate americano
55. al Park Safari
56. un Falcon (carro)
57. el Economist (periódico)
58. el Thanksgiving Day

III. Feminine in Spanish–Feminine in English

1. una engine (una turbina)
2. otra net (la red)
3. la guitarra de Pablo, a la Ovation
4. la green card
5. la Western Union
6. una flu—
7. la billboard (la cartelera)
8. la Standard Steel (la compañía)
9. la night
10. la British Airways
11. unas T-shirt
12. la high school (la escuela secundaria) (el bachillerato)?
13. la Texas Instruments
14. con una stripper (bailarina)
15. una book store
16. la Italian House
17. la Specializer noventa y cuatro (bicicleta)
18. la Phillips (calle? Compañía?)
19. la Economist (revista)
20. tu visa lottery: Oye, oye la, la mandaste

Bibliography

Alcoba, Santiago, and Julio Murillo. 1998. "Intonation in Spanish." *Intonation Systems. A Survey of Twenty Languages.* Ed. Daniel Hirst and Albert Di Cristo. Cambridge: Cambridge University Press.

Alonso, D., and V García Yebra. "El gallego-leaonés de Ancares y su interés para la dialectología portuguesa." *III Colóquio de estudos luso-brasileiros"* I: 331-65. Also in *CEG* 26: 43-79. (Cited by Porto Dapena, 1977.)

Anderson, Stephen. 1992. *A-morphous Morphology.* Cambridge: Cambridge University Press.

Anderson, Stephen R. 1993. "Wackernagel's Revenge: Clitics, Morphology, and the Syntax of Second Position." *Language* 69.1: 68-98.

Arteaga, Deborah L. 2000. "Articulatory Phonetics in the First Year Classroom." *MLJ* 84: 343-54.

Antilla, Arto and Young-mee Yu Cho. 1998. "Variation and Change in Optimality Theory." *Lingua* 104: 31-56.

Aronoff, Mark. 1994. *Morphology by Itself.* Cambridge, Mass.: MIT Press.

Bakovic, Eric. 2000. "Nasal Place Neutralization in Spanish." *ROA*. To appear in *U. Penn Working Papers in Linguistics* 1. Proceedings of the 24th Annual Penn Linguistics Colloquium.

___. 1996. "Foot Harmony and Quantitative Adjustments." *ROA* 96. Rutgers Optimality Archive. http://roa.rutgers.edu.

Bernhardt, B., and C. Stoel-Gammon. 1996. "Underspecification and Markedness in Normal and Disordered Phonological Development." *Children's Language.* Ed. C. Johnson and J. Gilbert. Vol. 9: 33-54.

Blevins, J. 1997. "Rules in Optimality Theory: Two case studies." *Derivations and Constraints in Phonology.* Ed. I. Rocca. Oxford: Oxford University Press. 227-260.

Bloomfield, Leonard. 1933. *Language.* New Cork: Henry Holt and Company.

Bosque, Ignacio and Manuel Pérez Fernández. 1987. *Diccionario inverso de la lengua española.* Madrid: Editorial Gredos.

Broselow, Ellen, Sue Chen, and Marie Huffman. 1997. "Syllable weight: convergence of phonology and phonetics." *Phonology* 14: 47-82.
Bybee, Joan, R. Perkins, and William Pagliuca. 1994. *The Evolution of Grammar: Tense, Aspect and Modality in the Languages of the World.* Chicago: University of Chicago Press.
Carballo Calero, Ricardo. 1979. *Gramática elemental del gallego común.* Vigo: Editorial Galaxia.
Carreira, María. 1985. "Spanish Stress Assignment, Plural Formation and Diminutive Formation." M.A. thesis, University of Illinois.
———. 1991. "The Alternating Diphthongs in Spanish: a Paradox Revisited." *Current Studies in Spanish Linguistics.* Ed. H. Campos and F. Martínez-Gil. Washington D.C.: Georgetown University Press.
———. 1992. "The Representation of Rising Diphthongs in Spanish." *Theoretical Analyses in Romance Linguistics.* Ed. C. Laeufer and T. A. Morgan. Vol. 74. Amsterdam: John Benjamins.
Castro, O. 1998. *Aproximación a la fonología y morfología gallegas.* New Orleans: University Press of the South.
Chomsky, N., and M. Halle. 1968. *The Sound Pattern of English.* New York: Harper and Row.
Colina, Sonia. 1995. "A constraint-based analysis of syllabification in Spanish, Catalan, and Galician." Ph.D dissertation, University of Illinois at Urbana-Champaign.
———. 1997. "Identity constraints and Spanish resyllabification." *Lingua* 103: 1-23.
Dressler, Wolfang U. 1985. "Typological Aspects of Natural Morphology." *Acta Linguistica Academiae Scientiarum Hungaricae* 35: 51-70.
Echols, C. and E. Newport. 1992. "The role of stress and position in determining first words." *Language Acquisition* 2: 189-220.
Crystal, D. 1969. *Prosodic Systems and Intonation in English.* Cambridge: Cambridge University Press.
Fant, L. 1984. *Estructura informativa en español. Estudio sintáctico y entonativo.* Stockholm: Almqvist and Wiksell International.
Fikkert, P. 1994. *On the Acquisition of Prosodic Structure.* Dordrecht: ICG Printing (HIL dissertations 6).
Ford, Alan and Rajendra Singh. 1994. "Quelques avantages d'une linguistique débarrasée de la morpho(pho)nologie." Conference presentation. Montréal Roundtable "Morphonology: Contemporary Responses," Montréal, September 30–October 2, 1994. *Trubetzkoy's Orphan: Proceedings of the Montréal Roundtable "Morphonology: Contemporary Responses."* Ed. Rajendra Singh and Richard Desrochers. Amsterdam: Benjamins 1996. 119-39.
Gillam, R., L. Hoffman, and A. van Kleeck. 1998. "Relationship between working memory and phonological awareness in children with SLI." Scientific Technical Presentation at the American Speech, Language, Hearing Association Annual Convention, San Antonio, TX.
Givon, T. 1979. *On Understanding Grammar.* New York: Academic Press.

Goldsmith, A. 1990. *Auto segmental and metrical phonology*. Malden, Mass.: Basil Blackwell, LTD.
Guitart, Jorge. 1997. "Variability, multilectalism, and the organization of phonology in Caribbean Spanish dialects." *Issues in the Phonology and Morphology of the Major Iberian Languages*. Ed. Fernando Martínez-Gil and Alonso Morales-Front. Georgetown University Press.
Halle, M., and J. R. Vergnaud. 1987. *An Essay on Stress*. Cambridge, Mass.: MIT Press.
Harris, James. 1969. *Spanish Phonology*. Cambridge, Mass.: MIT Press.
———. 1980. "Nonconcatenative Morphology and Spanish Plurals." *Journal of Linguistic Research* 1: 15-31.
———. 1983. *Syllable Structure and Stress in Spanish: A Nonlinear Analysis*. Linguistic Inquiry Monographs, Cambridge, Mass.: MIT Press.
———. 1985. "The Spanish Diphthongization and Stress: A Paradox Resolved." *Phonology Yearbook* 2: 31-45.
———. 1991a. "The exponence of gender in Spanish." *Linguistics Inquiry* 22: 27-62.
———. 1991b. "The form classes of Spanish substantives." *Yearbook of Morphology* 4. Dordrecht: Kluwer. Ed. G. Booij and J. van Marle. 65-88.
———. 1995. "Projection and edge marking in the computation of stress in Spanish." *A Handbook of Phonological Theory*. Ed. John Goldsmith. Oxford: Blackwell.
Hasegawa, Yoko. 1999. "Pitch Accent and Vowel Devoicing in Japanese." *Proceedings of the International Congress of Phonetic Sciences*. 523-26. Available as a PDF file at http://ist-socrates.berkeley.edu/~hasegawa/pub.html.
Hayes, S. C., and Aditi Lahiri. 1991. "Durationally-inspired intonation in English and Bengali." *Music, Language, Speech, and Brain*. Ed. Johan Sundberg, Lennart Nord, and Rolf Carlson. London: McMillan. 78-91.
Hayes, Bruce. 1995. *Metrical stress theory: Principles and case studies*. Chicago: University of Chicago Press.
Hirst, Daniel, and Albert Di Cristo. 1998. *Intonation Systems. A Survey of Twenty Languages*. Cambridge University Press.
Holt, Eric. 1997. "The Role of the Listener in the Historical Phonology of Spanish and Portuguese." *ROA* 278. http://roa.rutgers.edu.
Hooper, Joan B. 1976. *An Introduction to Natural Generative Phonology*. New York: Academic Press.
Hubbard, Kathleen. 1994. "Duration in Moraic Theory." Ph.D dissertation, University of California, Berkeley.
Hyman, Larry M. 1978. "Tone and/or accent." *Elements of Tone, Stress, and Intonation*. Ed. Donna Jo Napoli. Georgetown University Press.
Ito, Junko, Y. Kitagawa, and A. Mester. 1996. "Prosodic faithfulness and correspondence: Evidence from a Japanese argot." *Journal of East Asian Linguistics* 5: 217-239.

Jaeggli, Osvaldo. 1981. "Spanish Diminutives." *Contemporary Studies in Romance Languages.* Ed. F. H. Nuessel. Bloomington, Indiana: Indiana University Linguistics Club. 142-58.
Kager, René. 1992. "Are there any truly quantity-insensitive systems?" *BLS* 18: 123-32.
Kenstowicz, Michael. 1995. "Base Identity and Uniform Exponence: Alternatives to Cyclicity." *Current Trends in Phonology: Models and Methods.* Jacques Durand and Bernard Laks. Salford: European Studies Research Institute, University of Salford. 363-93.
Kiparsky, Paul. 1982. "Lexical Phonology and Morphology." *Linguistics in the Morning Calm.* Ed. The Linguistic Society of Korea. Seoul: Hanshin Publishing Company. 3-92.
———. 1994. "Allomorphy or Morphophonology?" Conference presentation. Montréal Roundtable "Morphonology: Contemporary Responses," Montréal, September 30–October 2, 1994. *Trubetzkoy's Orphan: Proceedings of the Montréal Roundtable "Morphonology: Contemporary Responses."* Ed. Rajendra Singh and Richard Desrochers. Amsterdam: Benjamins 1996. 12-31.
Lamontagne, Greg. 1996. "Relativized Contiguity." Part I: Contiguity and Syllable Prosody. *ROA* 150.
Larsen-Freeman, Diane, and Michael H. Long. 1991. *An Introduction to Second Language Acquisition Research.* New York: Longman.
Lathrop, Thomas. 1984. *Curso de gramática histórica española.* Barcelona: Ariel.
———. 1996. *The Evolution of Spanish. An Introductory Historical Grammar.* 3rd ed. Newark, Delaware: Juan de la Cuesta.
Leben, William. 1973. "Suprasegmental Phonology." Ph.D. thesis, MIT.
Levelt, Clara C., N. Schiller, and W. Levelt. 2000. "The Acquisition of Syllable Types." *Language Acquisition* 8.3: 237-64.
Liberman, M., and A. Prince. 1977. "On stress and linguistics rhythm." *Linguistic Inquiry* 8: 249-336.
Lleó, C., M. Prinz, C. El Mogharbel, and A. Maldonado. 1996. "Early Phonological Acquisition of German and Spanish: A Reinterpretation of the Continuity Issue Within the Principles and Parameters Model." *Children's Language.* Ed. C. Johnson and J. Gilbert. Vol. 9: 11-31.
Lloyd, Paul. 1987. *From Latin to Spanish.* Memoirs of the American Philosophical Society. Vol. 173. Philadelphia.
Lombardi, Linda. 2000. "Second language data and constraints on Manner: explaining substitutions for the English interdentals." *ROA.*
López Ornat, Susana, Almudena Fernández, Pilar Gallo, and Sonia Mariscal. 1994. *La adquisición de la lengua española.* México/Madrid: Siglo veintiuno editores, S.A.
Lozano, C. 1979. "Stop and spirant alternation: fortition and aspiration processes in Spanish Phonology." Ph.D dissertation, Ohio State University
Matthews, Meter. 1991. *Morphology.* Cambridge: Cambridge University Press.

Matluck, J. 1965. "Entonación hispánica." *Anuario de Letras* 5: 5-32.
McCarthy, John, and A. Prince. 1986. *Prosodic Morphology*. Ms., Brandeis University and University of Massachusetts Amherst. Corrected as *Prosodic Morphology 1986*. TR-32 Rutgers Center for Cognitive Science, Rutgers University.
___. 1993a. "Generalized alignment." *ROA*-7-0000 at http://ruccs.rutgers.edu/roa.html.
___. 1993b. "Generalized alignment". *Yearbook of Morphology*. Ed. G. Booij and J. van Marle. Dordrecht: Kluwer. 79-153
___. 1994. "Prosodic morphology." Parts 1 and 2: Prosodic morphology workshop. Utrecht: OTS.
___. 1995. "Faithfulness and reduplicative identity." *University of Massachusetts Occasional Papers* 18: 249-384.
Menéndez Pidal, R. 1973. *Mis páginas preferidas (Temas lingüísticos e históricos)*. Madrid: Editorial Gredos, S.A.
Morris, R. 2000. "Constraint interaction in Spanish /s/-aspiration: Three peninsular varieties." *Hispanic Linguistics at the Turn of the Millennium. Papers from the Third Hispanic Linguistics Symposium*. Ed. Hector Campos, E. Herburger, A. Morales-Front, and T. Walsh. Somerville, Mass.: Cascadilla Press.
Navarro Tomás, T. 1939. "El grupo fónico como unidad melódica." *Revista de filología hispánica* 1: 3-19.
Nespor, M., and I. Vogel. 1986. *Prosodic Phonology*. Dordrecht: D. Reidel.
Pater, Joe. 1997. "Minimal Violation and Phonological Development." *Language Acquisition* 6.3: 201-53.
Pensado, J. L., and C. Pensado Ruiz. 1983. *Gueada y geada gallegas. Verba*. Anexo 21. Universidad de Santiago de Compostela.
Perlmutter, David. 1998. "Interfaces: Explanation of Allomorphy and the Architecture of Grammars." *Morphology and Its Relation to Phonology and Syntax*. Ed. Steven G. Lapointe, Diane Brentari, and Farrel Patrick. Stanford, California: CSLI Publications (Center for the Study of Language and Information). 307-38.
Pierrehumbert, J.B. 1980. "The Phonology and Phonetics of English Intonation." Ph.D. dissertation, MIT (published in 1988 by the IULC).
Porto Dapena, J. Álvaro. 1977. "El gallego hablado en la comarca ferrolana." *Verba*. Anejo 9. Universidad de Santiago de Compostela.
Prieto, Pilar. 1992. "Spanish Diminutive Formation." *Hispanic Linguistics* 5: 169-205.
Prince, Alan. 1980. "A metrical stress theory for Estonian quantity." *Linguistic Inquiry* 11: 511-62.
Prince, Alan, and Paul Smolensky. 1993. "Optimality Theory: Constraint Interaction in Generative Grammar." Ms. Rutgers University and University of Colorado, Boulder.
Quilis, Antonio. 1988. *Fonética acústica de la lengua española*. Madrid: Editorial Gredos.

Saco y Arce, J. A. 1868. *Gramática gallega.* Lugo: Imprenta de Soto Freire. 2nd ed. Orense: Gráficas Tanco, 1967.
Selkirk, E. 1986. "On derived domains in Sentence Phonology." *Phonology* 3: 371-405.
Singh, Rajendra. 1994 (1996). Comments on discussion section of conference presentation. Montréal Roundtable "Morphonology: Contemporary Responses," Montréal, September 30–October 2, 1994. *Trubetzkoy's Orphan: Proceedings of the Montréal Roundtable "Morphonology: Contemporary Responses."* Ed. Rajendra Singh and Richard Desrochers. Amsterdam: Benjamins.
___ and Richard Desrochers, eds. 1996. *Trubetzkoy's Orphan: Proceedings of the Montréal Roundtable "Morphonology: Contemporary Responses."* Amsterdam: Benjamins.
Slobin, Dan. 1973. "Cognitive prerequisites for the development of grammar." *Studies of Child Language Development.* Ed. Ferguson and Slobin. New York: Holt, Rinehart and Winston. 175-208.
Sparks, R., and L. Ganschow. 1993. "Searching for the cognitive locus in foreign language learning difficulties: Linking native and foreign language learning." *Modern Language Journal* 77: 289-302.
Tesar B., and Paul Smolensky. 2000. *Learnability in Optimality Theory.* Cambridge, Mass.: MIT Press.
Tiffou, E. 1994. "De l'autonomie de la morphophonologie." Conference presentation. Montréal Roundtable "Morphonology: Contemporary Responses," Montréal, September 30–October 2, 1994. *Trubetzkoy's Orphan: Proceedings of the Montréal Roundtable "Morphonology: Contemporary Responses."* Ed. Rajendra Singh and Richard Desrochers. Amsterdam: Benjamins.
Trigo, Rosario L. 1988. "On the Phonological Behavior and Derivation of Nasal Glides." Ph.D. dissertation, MIT.
Trubetzkoy, N. S. 1929. "Notes sur le'desinences du verb dans le langues tche tche nolesguiennes (caucasiques-orientales)." *BSL* 29: 152-71.
___. 1931. "Die phonologischen Systeme." *Travaux du Cercle Linguistique de Prague* 4: 96-116.
___. 1939. "Grundzüge der Phonologie." *Travaux du Cercle Linguistique de Prague* 7.
Valladares Núñez, M. 1892. *Elementos de gramática elemental.* 1st ed. Vigo: Editorial Galaxia, 1970.
Veny, Joan. 1993. "Visió histórica de la 'fortuna del fonema /x/' en catalá." *Actea* 2: 405-37.
Weinrich, Harold. 1968. *Estructura y función de los tiempos en el lenguaje.* Spanish version of F. Latorre. Madrid: Gredos, Biblioteca Románica Hispánica.
Wenk, B. J., and F. Wioland. 1982. "Is French really syllable-timed?" *JP* 10.2: 193.

Yip, Moira 1998. "Identity Avoidance in Phonology and Morphology." *Morphology and Its Relation to Phonology and Syntax*. Ed. Steven G. Lapointe, Diane Brentari, and Patrick Farrel. Stanford, California: CSLI Publications (Center for the Study of Language and Information). 216-46.

Author/Subject Index

AGAL: 38
Alcoba and Murillo: 48, 49n8
alternating diphthongs: ix, 2, 57-64, 71, 74, 84-85, 92
Andalusian Spanish: 26-27
Anderson: 4
Antilla and Cho: 8, 82, 85
Argentinian Spanish: 48, 108
Aronoff: x, 71-72
Arteaga: 103
aspiration (of s): 5, 15, 21-22, 27, 108
assimilation (nasal): 5
Bakovic: 29, 109-10
Bernhardt and Stoe-Gammon: 18
Blevins: 9
Bloomfield: 72
Brazilian Portuguese: 41
Broselow, Chen, and Huffman: 9-11
Bybee: 1, 3, 59
Carballo Calero: 40
Carreira: 4, 57, 53
Castilian: 38, 40, 46, 48-49, 105-11, 114
Castro: 4, 40, 94n5, 106, 109
Catalan: 105-14
Chomsky and Halle: 3
Colina: 10, 14-15, 26
CONCORD: 8
Correspondence Theory: 7, 109
Crystal: 103
deletion of s: 5-6, 21
DEP(Endency): 7, 109-10
European Portuguese: 41, 48
Evaluator (EVAL): 7
diachronic: ix, 1-2, 34

diminutive: 1, 4-6, 29, 36, 53-54, 54, 58, 61-94
diphthong: ix, 1-2, 57-68, 71-72, 74, 84-85, 92, 98, 101-02
Dressler: viii, 2, 6n6
Echols and Newport: 14
EVAL: 7
Faithfulness constraints: x, 2, 7, 9, 15, 89, 109-10
Fant: 41
Fikkert: 16
FILL: 7, 109-10
Ford and Singh: 4
Galician: 4, 6n3, 29-30, 38-49, 105-14
geadas: 105-14
Generative Theory: 8
Generator (GEN): 6-7
Gillam, Hoffman, and van Kleeck: 96
Givón: 3
Goldsmith: 72
Guitart: 108
Halle and Vergnaud: 10
Hasegawa: 39, 44
Harris: 4, 29, 33, 57, 70, 71, 84, 94n17
Hayes: 10, 16
Hirst and Di Cristo: 40
Holt: ix, 109
Hyman: 39
Hooper: 3
Hubbard: 9
IDENT(ity)-[F]: 7, 109-10
Instituto da Lingua Galega: 38
intonation: 33-49
Itô et al: 10

Jaeggli: 4, 86
Kager: 10
Kenstowicz: 10, 15
Kiparsky: 3, 5
Kitagawa: 10
Lamontagne: 10
Larsen-Freeman and Long: 95
Lathrop: 55n2
learnability: ix, 2, 105-14
Leben: 9, 20,
Levelt, Schiller, and Levelt: 10, 22
lexeme: 58, 70, 72, 80, 88, 90-91
Lexical Phonology: 3, 8
Liberman and Prince: 10
Lleó, Prinz, El Mogharbel, and Maldonado: 21, 22
Lloyd: 55n2
López Ornat: 13, 16-22, 28, 30n1, 58-61, 28, 91, 94n7
Lozano: 109
Matthews: 72
Matluck: 41
MAX: 7, 109-10, 114
McCarthy: 7, 10, 89, 105, 109-10
McCarthy and Prince: 6, 9, 10
Menéndez Pidal: 52
Mester: 10
minimal word: 13
moraic theory: 9
moras: 9-11, 16, 28
morphology: ix-x, 1-6, 8, 15, 51-55, 70-71, 82, 84, 90
    A-Morphous Morphology: 4
    Projection Morphology: 4
Morris: ix, 22, 108
native system: ix, 55-68
Natural Phonology: 3
Navarro Tomás: 41
Nespor and Vogel: 72
non-native system: ix, 55-68
Obligatory Contour Principle (OCP): 8, 16, 51-55, 59, 79
Optimality Theory (OT): ix, 2, 6, 7-11, 26, 76, 105
Pater: 10, 13-14, 16-18
Pensado Ruiz et al: 106, 109
Perlmutter: 8
Phonology: ix-x, 1-3, 6, 8, 15, 18, 33, 51-55, 71, 89-90, 96
Pierrehumbert: 39

Porto Dapena: 45
Prague Circle: 3
Prieto: 27
Prince and Smolensky: ix, 7, 9-10, 105, 109-10
Queadas: 105-14

Quilis: 41
Real Academia: 34-35
rhyme: 4, 13, 31, 75
Saco y Arce: 106
Singh: viii, 4, 6n5
Selkirk: 9
Slobin: 18
Sparks and Ganschow: 100
SPE: 4, 7
standard Spanish: 27-28, 38, 41, 44, 52
terminal marker: 17, 28, 86, 88, 94n15
Tesar and Smolensky: 105
Tiffou: viii
Trigo: 29
Trubetzkoy: 1-2
Ulaszyn, Henryk: 6n5
Valladares Nuñez: 106
velarization (nasal): 5
Veny: 106-07
Weinrich: 9
Wenk and Wioland: 41
Yip: 8, 53

About the Author

Obdulia Castro is a native of Pontevedra, Spain. She obtained her Licenciatura en Letras from the Universidad Católica Andrés Bello in Caracas, Venezuela; and her M. A. and Ph.D. in Spanish Linguistics from Georgetown University in Washington, D.C. She has taught Spanish language, linguistics and /or teaching methodology at Georgetown University, George Mason University, St. Lawrence University, and the University of Colorado at Boulder. She is currently a full-time member of the faculty in the Department of Modern and Classical Languages at Regis University in Denver, Colorado. She is the author of *Aproximación a la fonología y morfología gallega,* and her articles on Spanish linguistics, foreign language learning difficulties, and teaching methodology have appeared in a number of selected conference proceedings and academic journals such as *Hispania* and *Foreign Language Annals*.